PRAISE FOR BORN TO BE PUBLIC

"Comedic gold."

- *O, The Oprah Magazine*

"An impressive humorist with a voice all his own."

- *Kirkus Reviews*

"Greg Mania is one of the funniest up-and-coming writers cranking out work and he is finally releasing his laugh-out-loud memoir....Come for the laughs, stay for the heart-warming story of coming out in the most millennial way possible."

- *Electric Literature*

"Greg Mania is the Cheesecake Factory of writers, and I say that with the utmost reverence: extravagant, unapologetic, hilarious, and fucking good."

- **Lindy West, author of *Shrill* and *The Witches Are Coming***

"This book is a hilarious wonder. Not only does it prove that Greg Mania was, indeed, born to be a public (and beloved) icon, but also that he was born to be a celebrated writer. It's sheer delight."

- Alissa Nutting, author of *Tampa* and *Made for Love*

"Greg is so fucking funny. Can you say 'fuck' in a blurb? Sorry if you can't, I'll pay the FCC fine or whatever since there's really no other word to describe how funny he is. FUCK!!!"

- Megan Amram, author of *Science...For Her!* and Emmy-nominated writer for *The Simpsons*, *Parks and Recreation*, and NBC's *The Good Place*

"Greg Mania's *Born to Be Public* is a delightful coming-of-age memoir filled with poignance and deep self-reflection, plus "advice" no one should take but everyone can relate to. I felt charmed and beguiled by this fizzy triple-threat: a book that is smart, insightful, and so funny that I got annoyed with myself for laughing so much."

- Lindsay Hunter, author of *Eat Only When You're Hungry*

"*Born to Be Public* is the literary equivalent of the best mall hang ever. Greg's writing is so witty and so warm and so generous, that I'm actually livid he doesn't personally come with his book so I can hear him tell me more about his extraordinary life over Red Lobster cheesy biscuits. His ability to meld heart and humor is exactly why he's been able to carve out such a unique and incredible reputation as a writer and I am in awe of his honesty and ability to use ALL CAPS PERFECTLY. If you don't buy this book for yourself and everyone you've ever met, I'll be mad at you."

- Anne T. Donahue, author of *Nobody Cares*

"*Born to Be Public* is a funny, heartfelt memoir that will have you rooting for Greg so hard. I want to press it into the hands of anyone who is finding themselves and say: you are not alone."

- Blythe Roberson, author of *How to Date Men When You Hate Men*

"Greg Mania is the friend at the party with all the good stories, the one with preternatural wisdom, perfect comedic timing, and a VIP table at five nearby Olive Gardens. *Born to Be Public* is a rollicking, hilarious, and poignant ode to being young and striving in New York, to finding your tribe, your voice, and yourself."

- John Glynn, author of *Out East*

"Greg is incredibly talented and wildly funny. What a joy to see his first book unleashed upon the world! May it be the first of many. We need his voice, his vulnerability, his weirdness, his kindness, his silliness, and his strength. And his hair, obviously."

- Sara Benincasa, author of *Real Artists Have Day Jobs*

BORN TO BE PUBLIC

GREG MANIA

This book is for anyone who's ever said to me, "you should write a book."

This book is also for the guy at the airport Subway who didn't charge me for a refill on my Sprite yesterday.

AUTHOR'S NOTE

Although the experiences recounted in this book are real, the names and identifying characteristics of some individuals have been changed to protect the privacy and anonymity of those involved, and also because I still want to have friends after this book is published. But also, even *if* you did want to sue me, it would be a tremendous waste of your time and money because I don't fucking have anything, unless you're after a bunch of books and a kitchen drawer full of duck sauce packets. In some cases, I've combined the characteristics and incidents of different people into one composite character and compressed certain timelines with the goal of maintaining people's privacy while preserving the integrity of the book. Now, let's boogie.

CONTENTS

BORN
TO BE
PUBLIC

A MEMOIR

GREG
MANIA

INTRO: PROTOTYPE GREG M@NI@

Can you believe someone is paying me to write this 200,000-character Tweet?

I can't. I mean, as someone who tweeted "my kink is a lunch stipend" earlier today, I find it hard to believe I'm employed, period. My profile picture on LinkedIn contained an exposed nipple for an entire year. I've posted a picture of me eating pizza on the toilet before. Shame? I don't know her.

My social media presence has always been, well, let's go with eyebrow-raising. If you're reading this book, you probably already know that because I've turned into a self-fellating promotional nightmare on social media and probably begged you seven-hundred times to please buy a copy because I guess I'm stuck doing this writing thing until I definitely die an early death from choking on a garlic knot.

But that's not what I'm worried about. I worry about a lot of things: I wonder when karmic retribution will strike for that one time I ate a granola bar from a food drive donation bin. I wonder what would happen if my appendix spontaneously burst in the worst place possible, like a transatlantic flight. WHAT IF I'VE ACCIDENTALLY REPEATED A JOKE IN THIS BOOK? My head is a conveyor belt, churning out one worry after another. But, deep down, my biggest worry is not being able to produce something of value.

Sure, making someone laugh is valuable. I'm providing them a brief respite from whatever may be ailing them at the time, a chance to forget their troubles and throw their head back and laugh at a story about the time I took Ambien and bid on a seventeenth century chandelier on an online auction. Or the time I got vertigo at Home Depot. But what story can I tell that will inspire others to find their truth, all while laughing along the way to discover it?

I'm inspired by those who have successfully cultivated their unique online personalities. The Rob Delaneys. The Megan Amrams. The So Sad Todays of the world. The ones whose voices capture the attention of millions on the internet and go on to shape popular culture through TV, movies, and books. I loved *Catastrophe* with Rob Delaney. I can watch an episode of *The Good Place* or *Parks and Recreation* and know which joke Megan Amram wrote. Melissa Broder's books are ones I revisit often. These are the people who made me want to become a comedy writer. I needed to follow in their foot-steps. And I did. I created a character—an over-the-top, extended version of myself—I was able to develop a style and voice through, someone I was able to perform as. And I've never broke character since.

Until now.

1. PARIAH PRODIGY

Prom 2009: The first and last time I looked good in tiny sunglasses.

You might be wondering how an increasingly peculiar kid grew up to be an Internet Spectacle. Well, I was fucking weird growing up—and not just because I liked sauerkraut as a child.

Sure, I still do and say things that warrant my parents' thumb and forefinger meeting at the bridge between their nose and eyebrow, rubbing away the tension facilitated by shame, but, for the most part, they get me now. But that hasn't always been the case. When I was about ten, my mom overheard me saying the word "fuck," and made me go downstairs to repeat what I said to my dad. In third grade, during a field trip my class took to Manhattan, I had to be escorted out of a *Blue Man Group* performance because I wouldn't stop screaming—for reasons that escape me now—but I do remember my teacher repeatedly saying, "no, those aren't demons," while trying to calm me down in the lobby.

A penchant for the theatrical, more times than not punctuated by an unbridled display of histrionics, is a more-than-adequate way to describe how I was growing up. So, it shouldn't come as a surprise to you, dear reader, that I've decided to share my childhood with you through a three-act structure.

ACT I

I grew up in central New Jersey. New Jersey is ninety percent malls. It's what we're known for. Idaho has potatoes; we have malls. If you grew up in New Jersey, you were baptized in a mall fountain. I grew up in a small town right outside of Trenton in a Polish household with a set of immigrant parents and a brother eleven years older than me.

My brother, Andy, and I are first-generation Polish-Americans, so we grew up in a household that always remained only somewhat Americanized. When other kids in my first grade class were eating PB&Js for lunch, I was taking out a thermos filled with warm soup that was usually accompanied by something like rye bread and sausages. It wasn't unusual for me to unpack my lunch and find something akin to *gołąbki*, which made the notorious elementary lunch trade impossible for me; my prospects for acquiring string cheese were slim to none. I didn't know what Chips Ahoy tasted like until I was, like, NINE.

I was already on the radar of being made fun of because of my often-smelly lunches. No one would want to sit near me, nor would I be invited to sit with anyone else. I would beg my parents for lunch money just so I could fit in by eating the pizza and chicken nuggets that were offered to those who bought lunch at school. Sometimes they'd give me money to buy lunch, but most of the time I'd just sit there, bitter, that I wasn't receiving my daily serving of high fructose corn syrup.

I also had an interest in things that other kids didn't have an interest in: other kids were playing with Furbies, Beanie Babies, and other toys that fanned the flames of nineties nostalgia; I was putting my mother's sashes around my head and romping around the living room to ABBA. I loved anything and everything yellow. Most, if not all, of my toys were yellow. I wanted a yellow Volkswagen Beetle. I planted yellow daffodils in the garden with my parents. If it wasn't yellow? GOOD DAY.

My dad shaped my taste in music. Because he was a vinyl DJ in a small town in southwest Poland named Opole in his twenties, we always had music from The Rolling Stones, Led Zeppelin, Elton John, Cher, Stevie Wonder, The Bee Gees,

Donna Summer, you name it, blaring from the speakers at our house. My mom passed down her love of fashion to me.

I admit with pride that my parents are cooler than I'll ever be. They both grew up circulating the European club scene and serving some serious looks. My dad dressed like the fifth Beatle and my mom looked like an iconic noir actress from the fifties whose face would now be plastered on a bunch of tank tops at Forever 21.

Like father, like son.

My mom, coming to a graphic tee at a Forever 21 near you.

Even though I grew up with some cool parents, I was still being picked on and bullied in school because of my interests and the things I loved. I wasn't like every other boy who was into WWE, Batman, and any sort of activity that resulted in injury and/or bloodshed.

In third grade I (and almost every girl) was obsessed with those nineties chokers, the ones that were springy and lace-like and stretched to fit around your neck. I didn't own one, but I would double-loop the lanyard I wore around my neck in a way so that the second loop would fit snugly against my neck, similar to the choker look. One girl named Jessica called me out on it, in the middle of class, in front of everyone, when someone asked me why I wore my lanyard around my neck like that. She told them it was because I wanted to be a girl. I never wore my lanyard like that again, at least not in school or anywhere in public.

I started to tend to my hobbies and interests in the privacy of my own home, where my parents gladly entertained whatever loves I had at the time: Britney Spears, Pocahontas, anything that shimmered. Instead of going on play dates like my other classmates were doing, I stayed home to read *Ramona the Pest*. I was obsessed with the "easy, breezy, beautiful Cover Girl" jingle, and sang it so many times Cover Girl should have cut me a check. I owned *Spice World* on VHS and watched it at every chance I got. I had a Little Mermaid backpack in kindergarten when all of the other boys had Batman or Spider-Man backpacks. I always chose the female characters in video games. All the boys in my class would tease me and call me a girl. I didn't know why it was so odd to them that my childhood idols were girls. It didn't make sense to me. My mom even dressed me up as Snow White for Halloween in third grade. (No, I don't have a picture; yes, I'm just as upset as you are.)

If it isn't obvious to you by now, I was the flamboyant gay kid. I was the one whose homosexuality acted like a pheromone for kids who are looking to pick on someone, someone who would definitely be classified as "sensitive" by teachers. Mix all of the above into a little kid and you've got yourself the most coveted auction item in front of an audience full of bullies.

ACT II.

I knew I was gay for as long as I remember—I think I realized it in utero. I basically came out of my mother's womb on a Pride float. I didn't know that there was a word for how I felt as a young kid, but I knew I was different.

I had my first crush on a boy named Chris in third grade. I tended to always be shy at that age, but around Chris I was practically mute. I would do things like inch closer to him when we stood in line to go out for recess, or always ensure we would be paired together for an assignment by sitting nearby.

After I finally mustered enough courage, I decided to make my intentions known. One December, right before school let out for the holidays, I wanted him to know I liked him, so I slipped him a candy cane and a Christmas card in his homework folder during free-time when we were allowed to read and draw or talk quietly among ourselves. When school was dismissed later that afternoon, as we lined up to be picked up by our respective parents and guardians, Chris and his mom walked past me and his mom THANKED ME IN FRONT OF MY ENTIRE CLASS FOR GIVING CHRIS A CANDY CANE AND CHRISTMAS CARD.

I was mortified.

I don't think his mother knew that Chris was the only one who received a candy cane from me, but the whole class did because no one else went home with a candy cane that day. After I was unintentionally called out, I stared ahead in silent horror and wished I could crawl into a hole forever.

I was teased for the rest of the year because everyone basically knew I had a crush on a boy, even though no one knew exactly *what* that meant, just that it was weird or unusual, either because it was something they were not exposed to or were used to seeing. Chris also went from happily playing with me during recess to avoiding me not unlike how you avoid someone you went to high school with at the TGI Fridays in your hometown when everyone is home for the holidays. I was constantly being called a girl because the few friends I had (two) were girls. I almost exclusively talked about Britney Spears, Sailor Moon, and clip-on earrings.

The moment everyone knew.

I had a hard time making friends at this age. Not just because I was flamboyant and feminine, but also because of my interests. At that age, we didn't have the vocabulary that included words like "gay" or "queer" or anything relating to that identity marker yet, so I was, by default, labeled the "weird" kid.

In fifth grade, me and one of my classmates, Brittany, were placed in remedial math. After a while, Brittany and I ended up liking each other, even becoming friends. One day, after math, we decided to walk back to our regular class together. Before we turned the corner that would lead us down the hall to our classroom, Brittany asked me to stay behind, because she didn't want to enter our room at the same time. It would look like we were friends, she said, which I thought we were.

She thought nothing of it; she asked me to stay behind in the same cadence someone uses to ask if you have change for a twenty. I did, because I didn't want her to stop liking me. I watched her walk in, and then, after counting to ten, I came in after her.

ACT III.

Middle school was a nightmare. I was continually teased and being called a girl or gay because I became obsessed with dying my hair. You may recall that 2004 was the apex of DIY paint-on highlights, every show punctuated by commercials for Herbal Essences highlighting kits ("with a one-of-a-kind Color Guard formula that will show you exactly where those gorgeous streaks will appear!").

I begged my parents to get me my own kit from the drugstore. They weren't surprised when I wanted to experiment with my style as they were both equally flamboyant with theirs in their youth, so my mom came home with a box kit of paint-on highlights for me one day.

BRACE YOURSELF.

Thirteen-year-old me in Paris sporting paint-on highlights
from the box and an Old Navy shirt. I haven't been
allowed back in the city since.

I warned you. As out-of-style as they are now, I thought I was HOT SHIT with my highlights that made my head look like a coonskin cap. But my classmates just used my affinity for out-of-the-box highlights as fuel to tease me, calling me a fag and any slur under the sun a little gay boy hears in their formative years. My opposition to anything masculine wasn't the only thing that put a metaphorical "kick me" sign on my back.

I was also heavily bullied because I was a late-bloomer and lanky as fuck—I was shoved in the hallway, into lockers—and it made changing in front of the other boys for gym hell for me, so I often feigned a stomachache and sat in the nurse's office to avoid gym class. I was such a late-bloomer that I hit puberty, like, twenty minutes before writing this chapter. When most of the boys in my grade started developing muscles and bulk and competed to outperform each other in gym class, I opted for badminton. I was made fun of for my high-pitched voice, so I almost never raised my hand to speak in class, a concern my teachers always relayed to my parents during parent-teacher conferences.

My parents intervened a few times by going to the principal and guidance counselor—I spent about ninety percent of my childhood in a guidance counselor's office—and things simmered down in between bullies who would choose me to pick on before finding someone else to inflict misery on, but it was never for long. Another day, another bully.

I combated all of the bullying by turning to comedy. My brother had a TV in his room so when he was in college, I would sneak into his room and turn on channels like Bravo and watch a Kathy Griffin stand-up special. If I heard my parents coming up the stairs, I would quickly change the channel to whatever was airing on PBS.

It was my nirvana. I was introduced to other comedians like George Carlin, Joan Rivers, Margaret Cho, Janeane Garofalo, Whoopi Goldberg, and Paula Poundstone at an inappropriately young age, most of whom were responsible for greasing the wheels on my premature potty mouth. I became obsessed with the intellectual infrastructure of a Carlin joke that enhanced his already paramount punchlines. I took notice of why some words were funnier than others and how intonation can greatly accentuate the delivery of a joke. I became obsessed with the economy of words; I loved how certain words sounded as opposed to others, how word order mattered.

Sarcasm quickly became my best friend. When you're a scrawny kid with a high-pitched voice, your best defense against bullying is public humiliation.

Once, in math class, I was filing a graded math quiz into my Dixie Chicks folder and this bully named Jeremy hissed, "fuck you, fag" into my ear.

"Wow, that's three more words than I thought you knew," I retorted.

Cue laughter from nearby classmates.

This is how I started to deal with the bullying: I equipped myself with snarky comebacks inspired by the sharp-tongued comedy mavens I watched obsessively. I got better at carefully selecting string of words whose combination proved to be more lethal than any slur hurled my way. I'd collect my laughs and then map out an alternate exit for when school let out so I wouldn't be paid back in the form of physical abuse. As Joan Rivers once said: *it* doesn't get better; *you* get better.

And it did get better, ironically enough, in high school. I became best friends with a girl named Rachel Hendershott, whom I idolized from the moment we met.

Rachel had the type of moxie I wish I had. Everyone gravitated towards her. Once, when we were job hunting one summer, she applied to work at Build-a-Bear at the mall. Part of the application process was to stand over the railing, which overlooked the first floor, ring a large bell and shout, "I JUST APPLIED TO BUILD-A-BEAR WORKSHOP, AND I HOPE I GET THE JOB!" The point was to see if the candidate had the type of playful, confident personality one needed to possess to work there. Without even thinking, Rachel grabbed the bell, went out there, and shouted so loud that the mall banned Build-a-Bear from including this part of the application process for potential employees ever again. I never admired a person more, never wished I could be like someone more than in that moment, when I watched her confidently walk out into the crowded second floor of the mall and do something embarrassing and mortifying as if she was simply asked to pass the potato salad at dinner.

She was cast as the comedic lead in all our high school plays; she was Lawrence High's Tina Fey. I wanted to be just like her, because she made being funny seem so easy, and she also had the most infectious laugh that, to this day, automatically puts me in a good mood. Because of her involvement in it, I joined theater.

I already loved musical theater (SURPRISE) and wanted to be in *Chicago* on Broadway more than anything. I still do; however, I lack the talent to do so. (BUT, I do wear a lot of black. If they called me today and asked me to substitute for a chorus member who's out sick I'd be like, "what time?" and just roll my garment rack down to The Ambassador Theater on Forty-Ninth Street.)

I auditioned for as many plays and musicals as I could. The highlight of my high school theater career was when I was cast in an eighties musical, aptly titled *Back to the 80's*, as Rick Astley, one of the leads. I got to Rickroll the audience for three nights in a row. I ended my number with a split that brought the house down in an effort to divert the audience's attention away from my less-than-impressive vocal abilities. Listen, I could, kind of, pull of "Never Gonna Give You Up," but because my tenor voice was slowly starting to become a bass, my repertoire was limited.

I never got the lead in any musical, instead I started getting cast as the comedic relief in plays, the quirky sidekick everyone loves and wishes had their own spin-off. I was happy playing these roles because those types of characters are my favorite anyway. Who doesn't wish Karen and Jack from *Will and Grace* had their own spin-off? I'd let someone run over my foot with a Ford Focus if Titus from *The Unbreakable Kimmy Schmidt* got his own show. After getting cast in this role show after show, I quickly found a group of friends in theater with whom I remain close to this day—Rachel and I are still best friends—and my love of performing continued to grow long after high school.

2. TRAUMA, TRAUMA, TRAUMA, TRAUMA, TRAUMA CHAMELEON

I did eventually become a triple threat, just not in the sense I had hoped to become—an exceptional actor, singer, and dancer—but in the sense that I was diagnosed with depression, anxiety, and obsessive-compulsive disorder. Not as impressive, BUT AT LEAST I COULD TELL PEOPLE I WAS A MULTIHYPHENATE.

I wasn't officially diagnosed with anxiety and depression until later in life, even though I did frequently experience both as a kid, but when I was nine, I was diagnosed with the type of OCD Katie Couric would film a special on. I could have easily had a camera crew follow me around all day when I was ten while I obsessively checked the weather and looked out the window for any signs of a tornado. In central New Jersey, where the chance of a funnel cloud forming and touching the ground is about as high as the alcohol content in non-alcoholic beer. I was petrified of tornadoes to the point where I would miss so much school that I risked being held back because I refused to leave the house if I saw even one ominous looking cloud in the sky.

One day, towards the end of my fifth-grade year, an incoming thunderstorm caused the sky to turn pitch black. It was three p.m., only a half an hour until dismissal. I knew March through June was prime tornado season because the chance of warm air colliding with cold, dry air is highest in spring, ergo causing an updraft that results in a rotation if winds are strong enough (STANDARD KNOWLEDGE FOR A TEN-YEAR-OLD. I WAS LIKE DIVISION OF FRACTIONS WHO?). When I saw the sky turn black, I got clammy and pale; I started pacing around the classroom, right in the middle of my teacher, Mrs. Sosinkski, assigning homework. She paused to ask if I was okay. I ignored her, instead I ended up grabbing my backpack from the back of the classroom and ran out, straight out the door, and didn't stop running until I got home, which, luckily, was just up the street, not even two minutes away. I literally just ran out of school.

A few years ago, *Dateline* actually did air a special that followed the day-to-day lives of three adolescents diagnosed with OCD, specifically living with irrational phobias, in addition to reporting on new research that explained how the mind of a person living with this disorder operates on a chemical level. Under neurotypical circumstances (imagine being neurotypical), fear triggers a fight-or-flight response.

Once the presence of danger is no longer detected, the neurotypical mind basically sends a signal out along the lines of "the coast is clear." In a mind operating on irrational levels, such as mine and the kids whose lives were documented on the special, the maladaptive response does not register the signal which declares no credible threat. There are obviously a lot of different types of OCD, and each person living with it has their own individual set of triggers and ways of living with it. There are (usually) an assortment of events and/or factors that set in motion how OCD and panic disorders manifest in an individual. Mine was triggered—and ultimately was made worse—by a particularly traumatic event when I was in the fourth grade.

I went to a Halloween party at my school and decided to go into the haunted house they had transformed the home economics classroom into. I thought it would be fun to be gently spooked, but it turned out that the people they hired to scare us were so traumatizing that I literally got knocked on my ass. And I'm not the only one. Other kids threw up—some even fainted—from going through what turned out to be an extremely age-inappropriate Halloween event. They might as well have filled the haunted house with actual demons and/or people who drive with kayaks strapped to the top of their cars. I don't think I would even go through that haunted house now as a twenty-eight-year-old. No, thank you! Some parents even took legal action against my school. This event opened the floodgates for a slew of irrational fears to pour in, each coming and going as I moved through adolescence and into my teens.

I had my first panic attack at thirteen. As in, I couldn't breathe and didn't know what the fuck was happening. Now, when I have a panic attack, I just excuse myself to find a quiet place to close my eyes and count until it passes. I don't care where I am. If I'm with people I just say, "so I'm having a panic attack, please excuse me while I lock myself in the demo Kia Soul that's in this mall and I'll rejoin you all shortly. Please carry on!" But no one forgets their first panic attack.

My irrational fears at this age centered around my

parents. I was convinced they would die in a freak accident every time they left the house. I came home from school one day and noticed my mom's red minivan wasn't in the driveway. This wasn't unusual, because one of us usually followed the other since my day and hers ended at the same time. I had a key to the house and let myself in. I watched the clock slowly creep past four, still no sign of her red Plymouth. Only ten minutes had gone by, but, to my mind, it felt like an eternity.

I started to feel a constricting feeling in my throat, like I was being choked by a phantom. My mind wouldn't stop racing, a loss of control taking over my mind and body, a sense of doom amplifying by the minute. Then, of course, it started to pour. My mind was churning out every worst-case scenario possible like a bill counting machine. I kept calling her cell phone, but she didn't answer. I tried calling the elderly woman she was a nurse aid for, and she told me my mom had left not too long ago, that I shouldn't worry, she'd be home soon. I was like, PROBABLY NOT. GUESS THIS IS HOW I DIE.

The panic consumed me. I wanted to rip my skin off, just to regain some sense of control. A few minutes later, my mom came home. She was stuck in traffic and heard her phone ringing, but she couldn't answer because her cell phone clip broke and she couldn't pry her phone out. I was shaken up over that day for a good few weeks. And it wouldn't be the last time I spiraled out of control over something minor because my brain wasn't letting me compute what was happening around me in a rational progression of thought.

It got the point where my parents' lives were not just affected by their overwhelming concern for me, but they also couldn't enjoy the things they liked to normally do out of fear of me having an "episode" every time they tried to leave to the house. One time they left me with my brother while they went furniture shopping and my brother had to spend two hours calming me down.

My parents had to take turns by going in late to work, or leaving early, or taking off from work altogether, just to give me a sense of security. If I was at school and felt a panic attack coming on, I would immediately go to the nurse's office where I claimed to have a headache. Then I'd call one of my parents and ask them to pick me up. But, like clockwork, as this irrational phobia started to fade, another one was just around the corner like, "SURPRISE, BITCH, I BET YOU THOUGHT YOU'D SEEN THE LAST OF ME."

I'm fourteen, unable to sleep a wink because I'm convinced our house would be burglarized in the middle of the night. Every little noise—the house settling, our cat, Oliver, roaming about, the trees outside swaying in the wind—sent a shock down my spine. Let me provide you with a little context regarding our neighborhood, or I should say lack thereof. On one side, we have our neighbor, who actually happens to be my cousin Chris, and his family. On the other side, we have our other neighbors, with a road leading to the intermediate school, where I attended grades four through six, dividing the properties. Across the street from our house is THE DEPARTMENT OF MILITARY AND VETERAN'S AFFAIRS, WHICH HAS AROUND-THE-CLOCK SECURITY. And next door to that? The Army National Guard. Can we please applaud my parents' patience every time I would beg them to please install a security system? How they didn't shout, "NO ONE IS GOING TO TRY TO BREAK IN TO STEAL YOUR VHS TAPE OF *SPICE*

WORLD AND A BOP-IT WHEN WE LIVE ACROSS THE STREET FROM THE BITE-SIZED VERSION OF THE PENTAGON" is beyond me. I'm fairly certain if we'd stuck up one of those signs that warn possible intruders that the house is protected by a security system, the employees from the building across the street would take turns slow-clapping at us.

As I grew older, I knew, logically, that my fears were unfounded, yet because of my inability to receive the signal to confirm that logic, I continued to panic. But I didn't have that logic at that age. I felt like a hostage restricted to the confines of my own mental capacity, sequestered to a place in my mind I didn't know existed that churned and ruminated on scenarios I knew wouldn't come to fruition, yet terrified of the non-existent chance they would.

My parents tried, repeatedly, to seek professional help. We went through therapist after therapist, each session ending in tears and a refusal to go back. I hated therapy as an adolescent. It's like every time I was forced to talk about my problems, they became real to me, and I preferred to ignore them, which, only made it worse. It also augmented the differences I already thought made me an outlier among my classmates, which were my femininity and interests in things that weren't deemed "normal" for boys to like. Going to see someone to talk about my problems—an irrational fear of weather, sleeping in my parents' bed as an eleven-year-old because it felt like the safest place to be in case of a home invasion—felt like a cosmic joke the universe was playing on me.

But I grew up and attend therapy regularly now. Sometimes twice a week (not to brag). Therapy literally saved my life. I still struggle, but I've learned coping skills to ride out the worst moments. And they are rough: they're darker and more complex now and bring on certain anxiety-related disorders like dissociation and depersonalization. Disassociating is particularly unpleasant, because it entails a feeling of leaving your physical body and hovering over it, almost as though you're looking down on yourself. Periods of extreme stress and anxiety cause me to disassociate, so that's why you'll never catch me participating in Black Friday. Sometimes I'll lie awake at night wondering why I can't stop thinking about death or certain other cheerful topics. WHY SLEEP WHEN YOU CAN READ ABOUT THE HEAT DEATH OF THE UNIVERSE UNTIL TWO IN THE MORNING?

In addition to therapy, I've read countless books, learning about each disorder and teaching myself how to live with them. I believe knowledge is best way to approach mental illness upon diagnosis of having one. It's like each mental illness is in a relay race and I'm the shiny baton they pass to one another. When I'm not battling overwhelming bouts of depression, where it takes me an incredible amount of energy to leave the house or compete the simplest tasks like doing the dishes or cleaning my apartment, I'm fighting crippling anxiety that scratches at my brain not unlike a dog who is ready to be let in. And if it's none of the above, I'm drowning in a sea of obsessive thoughts that feel like they'll consume me whole. I've also recently been diagnosed with Post-Trau-matic Stress Disorder (PTSD), following a fire in my old apartment building.

And it's not all mental. Stress and trauma can trigger physical pain in the body, resulting in chronic pain and inhibiting normal bodily functions. These symptoms can go on to form a symbiotic relationship between the mental and physical, one affecting the other, to the point where sometimes my physical pain can make me depressed, and my depression can sometimes result in physical pain. This manifestation is new to me, and my body. I have to remember to be kind to myself, that I won't find the balance to operate at a normal capacity every day.

And that's okay.

Being able to admit I'm struggling makes me open to talking about how I'm feeling, and it doesn't come at the sake of my agency, which is a misconception many retain about allowing yourself to be vulnerable. In fact, it's the opposite. And sometimes finding the strength that comes with letting my guard down is just enough to help me make it to the next day. I'm thankful for my vulnerability.

Don't be fooled: I'm not someone who keeps a gratitude journal. If you do, that's great; I admire you and your desire to log the things you feel blessed by. But if you gifted me a gratitude journal, it would probably end up wedged between two overdue library books under my bed. A former roommate of mine once put up a motivational poster that read "Think like a proton: always positive," which caused me to contemplate arson. I thrive on negativity. Complaining is my favorite pastime; it's the one thing I'd list I'm grateful for if I did have a gratitude journal. Not very redeeming qualities—I know!— but at least by embracing *all* the parts of me—the totality of me—I'm able to accept the parts of me I had, at one point, felt cursed with.

3. LIKE A LAMPSHADE IN A FRAT HOUSE

My path to self-discovery started in college. I got accepted to Hofstra University and moved to Long Island to pursue an undeclared major in 2009. Hofstra is known for a number of things: it's a nationally recognized arboretum; it's hosted a slew of presidential debates; and it deploys a large number of Santas that are probably a major reason why so many bartenders in NYC hate SantaCon. But, back in 2009, I only cared about one thing: being close to New York City.

Living on my own—well, with a roommate who was definitely the type of straight dude who would deploy a meme thematically akin to something like "Cinco de Drinko"—and so close to NYC made everything feel ripe with possibility. I wanted to explore my voice in a way that I couldn't in high school. I enrolled in a creative writing class and wrote about my first time going to a gay club the summer before college, which you'll read more about in the following chapter. I detailed the fog, the lights, the atmosphere, the freedom, the liberation that came from grinding up with a hot, older man, relishing in the anonymity that was protected by the boundaries of the dance floor.

I wrote about finding a space to dance to the type of music I would have, in any other space, found uncomfortable dancing to, scared that I would attract the wrong kind of attention that could possibly result in a slur or some sort of retribution. My love of pop music was not only shared in the place I was writing about, but it was basically mandatory. Thank Gaga.

Pat, my professor for that class, quickly became my mentor after seeing potential in me that I didn't know existed. She made me believe in my talent as a writer and helped hone the skills I thought I didn't have. She encouraged me to explore my voice instead of trying to shape it into the cookie-cutter academic tongue that many of my teachers in high school tried to equip me with. I was finally beginning to discover my voice on the page. It was growing along with my confidence, my hair, and an incipient collection of leather jackets and ostentatious footwear.

She told me to write something that was me, something that I would want to read. She told me if I enjoyed writing it, someone out there would enjoy reading it.

I started writing a comedy blog called *Le Cabaret De Mania*. I also joined Twitter, which is a great way to learn about the art of brevity and using those limitations to your advantage when structuring a joke. I wrote about everything on my blog: funny things that happened to me or around me, like the time I gifted my mom Chanel perfume for Christmas and she used it as an air freshener in the bathroom because she ran out of Febreeze, pictures of outfits I've procured from thrift stores, and stories about my introduction to New York City nightlife, which I started exploring since Manhattan was just a half-hour train ride away.

I started going out to gay clubs and seedy dive bars that will serve you as long as you don't look twelve. At first, I only wore a T-shirt and some jeans to go out. But after seeing the characters populating the bar and dancefloors, I started styling my hair in a mohawk and wearing leopard-sequin tights to class, earning me many-a-double-take and side glances from students and faculty alike. I was absorbing New York's rock n'roll dive bar scene by night and pursuing a college degree by day.

I was basically living a double life, even though I didn't bother to look like it. There was no Clark Kent to my Superman, no disguises, even though as a gay boy I coveted every outfit Jennifer Garner wore in *Alias*. BITCH, REMEMBER THAT RED WIG? TO DIE FOR. But I was trying to be two people at once, which just made it harder to unearth the core of who I was.

I found the beauty in being an academic *and* someone who decided to incorporate fishnet gloves into their everyday attire. But there was still a dislocation in trying to reconcile these two parts of me, and it only delayed my actualization of self. I tried so hard to fit in, in both worlds, which just ended up making me greatly unhappy, especially as a fledgling freshman who thought the freedom of living away from home for the first time would just magically unlock the door I could never previously open. I realized I was wasting time trying to reconcile two parts that didn't need reconciling. They could co-exist, for my sense of self is a totality of these different parts. I didn't have to hide certain parts of me anymore.

I learned this lesson by following in the footsteps of one my comedy idols after reading her memoir, *Like a Lampshade in a Whorehouse.* If you're one of those heathens who will be part of the graduating class of 2025, who doesn't know what a dial tone sounds like nor doesn't remember the show *Holly-wood Squares,* chances are you don't know who Phyllis Diller was. Let this grandpa fill you in.

Phyllis Diller was a groundbreaking stand-up comedian who paved the way for people like Joan Rivers, Ellen DeGeneres, and a number of other female comics you know and love today. She was known for her self-deprecating stage persona, loud, shimmering, over-the-top fashion, giant blonde hair that could be seen from space, with a cackling laugh to boot. Her career spanned for more than fifty years, from making her television debut in 1958 as a contestant on Groucho Marx's quiz show *You Bet Your Life* to starring in movies alongside fellow comedy icon Bob Hope to guest-star-ring on a million shows including *The Muppet Show, The Love Boat, 7ᵗʰ Heaven,* and *The Drew Carrey Show*

I first discovered her in animated form on *Scooby-Doo,* and I immediately fell in love with her voice, which ignited my love for the seminal comedian.

I loved how she used her garish ensemble to propel her unique brand of humor. Comedically, our styles are polar opposites: her jokes were punchline-driven and mine tend to be on the opposite end of the spectrum, following the struc-ture a raconteur might employ. It was her story, chronicled in her memoir that I mentioned earlier (that I would swear in on if I were ever elected into Congress), *Like a Lampshade in a Whorehouse,* that earned her a number one spot in my hero Rolodex.

She forged her own space, her own legacy. She fit in by not fitting in and paved the way for so many others whom I idolize. I wanted to be just like that, except throw in a little Courtney Love and Elton John. That was the space I wanted to claim for myself, even if I didn't yet fully understand nor comprehend how doing so would unfold for me professionally down the road. But when you're seventeen, eighteen, nineteen, you're still learning who you are, so in that regard, I was right on track.

If you think about it, I made no sense—it's like meeting a gay Republican. I was dressing as if Billy Idol and Liberace had a son, but my writing was eighty percent comprised of stupid jokes and anecdotes about the time I threw up at Pottery Barn Kids. But that's the thing: identity is never neat. It's messy, ever-changing, grainy, unpredictable, frenetic, all over the place, and we'll never be able to reconcile ourselves because we're not supposed to. Every time we think we have ourselves figured out, we go and change again.

4. (SEXUAL) ORIENTATION WEEK

I had a crush on approximately 72,000 boys on campus. My first college crush was on a dude named Steve, who lived a few floors above me in the high-rise I lived in freshmen year. He said hi to me in the elevator once and I responded with, "yes."

...

...

...

MURDER ME.

After Steve, there was Alex, then Tyler, then Adam, and so on and so forth because I can't even remember all the dudes I drunkenly messaged on Facebook at three in the morning. I was drawing rejections like UNO cards before long. But before any of these boys, there was Jason, my first posting-antsy-lyrics-about-wanting-someone-who-doesn't-even-know-I-exist-and-even-if-he-did-he-would-never-go-for-someone-like-me-as-my-AIM-away-message crush during my senior year of high school.

James and I were in the same theater company. "Of

course," says you. He was the rising star of our high school's theater program, getting cast as the lead in *Fiddler on the Roof* as just a freshman. We didn't run in the same social circles outside of theater since he was a year younger than me and had his own group of friends, and likewise for me, but we did get to hang out during rehearsals for the fall play and spring musical.

During the spring of my senior year, when we were rehearsing for *Back to the 80's*—yes, the same one where I Rick—rolled the audience, I started to develop a serious crush on James. It wasn't an overnight thing. I've always thought he was cute, but I didn't allow myself to think it let alone do anything about it. But when we started spending every day after school together, rehearsing, I couldn't stop thinking about how much I liked him.

As my feelings intensified, so did my urge to tell someone because HELLO, what's the fun of having a crush if you can't analyze it with someone else?! I told one of my closest friends, Allison, first. She embraced me and told me how happy she was that I could share this with her, and she even gave me advice on how to talk to James. She suggested I instant message him on AIM and ask him something innocuous, like how his weekend was going or what his plans were for the summer.

The relief I felt telling someone about my crush was euphoric; I told my other best friends, like Rachel and my other friend, Danielle, who were just as supportive and loving as Allison. With encouragement from my friends, I started chatting with James on AIM, talking about theater and musicals we liked, music we listened to. One day, he posted something on Facebook asking if anyone wanted to go see his cousin's play over at The College of New Jersey. I decided to nonchalantly message him on AIM, seven seconds later: "HEY WHAT'S UP I'M SO BORED PLANS TONIGHT?" Just as I'd hoped, he asked me if I wanted to go see his cousin's play.

I was overjoyed. The whole night I felt a buzzing in my chest, evidence of the state of euphoria I was in. I came home that night and texted every single detail to my trio of friends: "he looked really cute"; "he said we should go see another show together soon!"; "I think his eyes lingered on my lips for a second!!!!". Of course, I still didn't know if he liked me like that, but every time we hung out, just the two of us, my crush escalated to the point where I thought that if I didn't tell him I would implode.

Telling him myself was out of the question, so, like a celebrity leaking some juicy story on TMZ in an effort to get publicity, I had my friend Danielle leak the news since I knew she was friends with him. She agreed to tell James over AIM that I had a crush on him, but, with my explicit instructions, tell him that I had no idea she was telling him my secret so that he could initiate the conversation so I wouldn't have to. LISTEN, I WAS THE BRAND AMBASSADOR OF AWKWARD.

I assumed he would return my feelings: he would approach me, either in person or message me on AIM, and we would end up secretly dating, sneaking each other sly glances in the hallway when we passed each other, holding hands in the wings of the stage during rehearsal in the dark, making out in his green Subaru in some dark parking lot, up until we would decide to no longer keep our relationship a secret anymore, that we would be openly proud to be each other's boyfriend and that we wanted to show our love to the world. We would arrive at prom together and everyone would slowly turn around, smile and cheer, and then the credits would roll across the bottom of the screen while Freeform introduced the next midday Saturday feature.

Turns out that's not what happened at all. He told Danielle, on AIM, that if I liked him, I should tell him myself —THAT WASN'T IN THE PLAN—so I went into teenage triage while I tried to figure out what to do next.

Eventually, I couldn't take it anymore and told him myself over AIM one weekend. He said that although he didn't return my feelings for him, he still wanted to be friends. I was crushed, but I was happy that he still wanted to hang out with me. He then went on to tell me that he especially valued my friendship because he didn't have any other gay friends—he was only out to a select few, too—and with that, proposed we go out and meet other gay people sometime. I wondered when and where he had in mind until one summer, the summer before I would leave for college and when we both turned eighteen (he was a year older than everyone else in his class), he asked me if I wanted to go to a gay club in Philadelphia that had an eighteen-and-up night.

I still very much had a crush on James at the time, so the summer before college, when he asked me if I wanted to go to Woody's, a popular gay club in Philadelphia that hosted an eighteen-and-up night on Wednesdays, I said yes. I thought, naively, that if we went to a club together, he would see me in a new (strobe) light, and then realize he had made a mistake and want to be with me. LOL AT ME FOREVER. Even though I said yes, I was nervous about how I would pull off going to a gay nightclub in Philadelphia.

I didn't know what to tell my parents. I ended up making a story about going to a sleepover that a friend from theater decided to have for the whole company before all the seniors went away for college. They believed me, especially when they saw James, whom they recognized from every show, pick me up in front of our house. I felt like I was doing something illegal; I was antsy for the entire drive to Philadelphia. I didn't know what to expect, and I was nervous that my parents would somehow find out I wasn't at the fictional sleepover where I said I'd be.

After we parked and walked over to Woody's, I became widely cognizant of the fact that, even though it was eighteen-and-up that night, we were the youngest people there. Maybe it's because we just looked young, but everyone there was dressed as if they were going to the club; we looked as if we were going to Denny's at two in the afternoon. After getting our IDs checked, we went upstairs, and because we couldn't be served alcohol, stood by the wall while we watched everyone laughing and dancing and having a good time.

Sensing the tension, James asked if we should just rip the band-aid off and just start dancing. I was mortified—and sober!—but I didn't know what to say, so I panicked and agreed. Luckily, Britney's "Toxic" came on just as we were making our way to the dance floor, buoying my confidence enough to plunge into the sea of dancing people.

It felt awkward at first, just James and me dancing, not even together, but like two platonic friends who decided to be each other's date to a wedding, but within moments two older-looking men came over and started dancing with us. It was my first time receiving and interacting with male attention like this: at first, I didn't know how to respond. I'm sure I danced with the grace of a drunk water buffalo, but once the man I was dancing with put his hands on my hips, I was transported to another world. It felt like an out-of-body experience, as if I were watching some alternate reality unfold before my eyes, mostly because I never dreamed that I would find myself at a gay club, grinding up against another guy, when just a few months ago I could barely tell anyone about my feelings for another boy.

By around two in the morning, we were sweaty and exhausted from all the dancing, and finally decided to drive home. We were about to leave until we heard "Poker Face" come on, and James, knowing that I loved Lady Gaga, asked me if I wanted to stay for one more song. I was already on the dance floor before he could even finish asking.

I wanted to actually kiss a boy. I wanted physical intimacy. As the fall semester at Hofstra progressed, so did my quest for coitus. A bunch of friends I made at Orientation Week and I decided to hop on the Long Island Rail Road into Manhattan to see what our underage options were off-campus. We ended up going to a now-defunct gay club called Rush, the one Saturday night a month that was eighteen-and-up, just a few weeks into the semester. Rush was much smaller than Woody's, but the energy and excitement was just as palpable.

I scanned the crowd looking for a cute guy, but every time one even made eye contact with me, I would start dancing like Ally Sheedy in *The Breakfast Club*. And even if someone did want to dance with the arm-flailing inflatable tube man that found itself into a gay club, I would panic and deflect any moves they made. I wasn't ready for such a public display of affection, as much as I wanted it, but it was like going from zero to sixty. I needed to take baby steps. I left that night disappointed—mostly in myself—but I wouldn't have to wait long for another chance to present itself to me again.

My first kiss ended up being with a boy I went to high school with. I was home for winter break a few weeks later, and I went to a house party a fellow LHS alum was throwing.

I was wasted on vodka and Luke, a boy who was a year younger than us, showed up. I heard rumors that he was gay, which were confirmed five minutes later in the hallway bathroom, when his tongue was in my mouth.

I would make out with many boys, in many bathrooms in the years to come, but since this was my first time kissing a boy, it's no surprise that this moment stands out among dozens like it to follow. It felt like a breakthrough. I finally knew what it was like to kiss a boy, and it felt right. If this was what being gay was like, I was like I'M IN BITCH. We didn't do anything other than kiss, and it wouldn't be until the fall semester of my sophomore year, almost a year later, that I had my first sexual experience.

My editor wants me to go into detail about my first time having sex, but honestly it was about as memorable as that minor cold you had in 2008. I know this is going to sound bad, but sex, to me, wasn't a Special Event. I tossed my virginity away as if it were a pair of old of sneakers that I was ready to part with.

It was a one-night stand.

There was a trifecta of popular bars near Hofstra: Dizzy's, Nacho's, and McHebes, all a hop and a skip away from each other on the Hempstead Turnpike. If you're going to a bar that's on a highway, you will get—and I can't stress this enough—staph. They will also definitely not card you. I was coming home from one of the three, drunk off of intensely hued cocktails named something like "Orange Cyclone." After swiping into the gate on the south side of campus with my school ID card, my friend and I, visibly inebriated, bumped—literally, I fell to the ground because I'm a paragon of finesse—into a boy on his way out to one of the bars on what I, lovingly, referred to as the Hempstead Strip.

The three of us made small talk that resulted in us exchanging numbers and promising to "hang out sometime," which, in any other situation, would be a legitimate a promise as the promise you make to hang out and catch up with that person you took AP U.S. History with in high school that you randomly happened to bump into on the train on your way home from work—but this time was the exception.

A few hours later, I was mid-bite eating a sandwich when he texted me that he just got home and would I like to come over and hang out? I knew what was going to happen; he knew what was going to happen. Even the most socially inept, and I'm including myself in that category, know that if someone is making plans with someone past a certain late-night/early-morning hour, you're going to see each other naked.

I put the rest of my sandwich in my mini fridge, paused the episode of *Charmed* I was watching, and went over to his dorm. After I signed into his building, he led me into his room, where he proceeded to put some music on. Since this was my first time, I didn't know what to do. I should kiss him, right? Or does he make the first move? Would he notice if I pulled up a wikiHow on my phone? Thankfully, he made the first move.

He started kissing me and fiddling with my belt buckle. I followed his lead and undid his. What followed was a bunch of awkward gyrating, gratuitous use of the phrase "does that feel OK?", and an unwelcomed use of teeth. After some disappointing oral, it was time for penetration—at least according to the porn I watched.

I didn't know if I was a "top" or a "bottom," nor do I know how we would determine that. Do we flip a coin? What if we're *both* tops or *both* bottoms; does that mean we would have to fight to the death? Would my astrological chart determine a proclivity towards one more than the other? I realize I did not do as much research as I should have before this step. What was I supposed to do now, *communicate?*

Before I could open my mouth to seductively ask "SO WHAT NOW?", I felt his dick poking around below, him repeatedly asking me, "is it in?" The lights were off, because at that point, that was my only kink. There was no way I was going to engage in intercourse with the lights on. I even unplugged his nightlight by the door. I don't need anyone to see that I forgot to pluck the hair from that one mole on my chest, or that I have a blackhead forming in one of my blind spots. Finally, he JAMMED IT IN AND PROCEEDED TO POUND INTO ME LIKE SOMEONE FRANTI-CALLY PRESSING THE CLOSE DOOR BUTTON IN AN ELEVATOR. He finished before I could even get used to him being inside me. It lasted for all but two minutes, and even that's being generous. In my head I thought, "*that's* sex? I WANT A REFUND." After a few minutes of lying side by side in his bed, he asked if I wanted to go again.

I'm pretty sure my MacBook didn't even go to sleep by the time I got back to my room to resume my episode of *Charmed.*

At this point, I was out to everyone—except my family back home.

My coming-out-to-my-family story is probably unlike any other, mostly because Google outed me. I was an open book to the world, the internet—essentially an endless chasm of strangers—before I could even offer a glimpse of my authentic self to the people who knew me better than anyone else. I was the opposite of what my family valued, which is, above most things, privacy; I'll tell the person I'm sharing an UberPool with that I'm uncircumcised. But beyond that, I was sharing photos of me in ripped tights, wearing a visible G-string, writing about the boys I had crushes on, speaking a member of One Direction sitting on my face into existence— basically treating the internet like a glorified diary.

I came home one day from college and my parents told me they googled me, saw the pictures, my blog, and veritably asked me if I was gay. Even though I didn't explicitly say yes, I also didn't say no. I was blindsided; I wasn't prepared to enter this territory, not yet. I shrugged my arms and went upstairs to my room, a feeling of unease hovering over the house for the whole weekend.

We didn't really talk about it after that initial interaction, probably because I figured we both needed time to sort out our feelings. My mom and dad, however, eventually sat me down to tell me that they would love me no matter what, and that made me a little less anxious about the outcome I was initially terrified of.

After a while, I understood that they started to google me to get the answers from the questions about my life that I was constantly dodging. They were the last to know about every-thing happening in my life, and I came to understand how that would hurt a parent who just wants to be involved in their child's life, who hopes their kid feels like they can share anything with them. I was scared to come out; I was scared of what their reaction would be because at the end of the day, no matter who we are or what secret about our identity we're hiding, we just want the people who love us to keep on loving us.

They would see me coming home with my laundry and

would come across things like mesh shirts, leopard-print pants from Trash and Vaudeville, and crop-tops with Debbie Harry's face on them—ostensibly they had questions. They also knew that I had a blog but didn't know whom or what I was writing about. Curiosity lead to them searching my name on the internet and coming across my blog and pictures. When I finally told them everything, about how I was gay, that I wanted to be a writer and a comedian, here's how the exchange went down:

My parents when I told them I'm gay: "Who cares?! We love you no matter what and we just want you to be happy!"

My parents when I told them I want to be a comedian: "Oh, well, how do you know you're not into business administration or nuclear engineering if you've never tried it?!"

When you're coming out, and it doesn't have to necessarily be coming out as someone who is LGBTQ+, it can be whatever change you want to make in your life, the question you're asking the people you love is, "will you still love me if...?," and it's not knowing the answer to that question that scares us. I know many aren't fortunate when it comes to having an accepting family, but that's the beauty of choosing your own family. I am a member of someone's chosen family and vice versa. There will always be someone out there who loves you and will encourage you to be unapologetically you. If you're fearful of whether you'll still be loved after coming out, know that someone, somewhere will always be there to say "yes."

5. YES, THAT'S MY REAL LAST NAME

Actively seeking well-known NYC socialites via social media and trying to get their attention in a shameless fashion by posting exhibitionistic content ranging from borderline crude humor to eyebrow-raising photos: Effective? Yes. Morally questionable? Perhaps. Shallow? Great opportunity for a duet at karaoke.

I was already spending multiple nights a week traipsing to Manhattan, which was only a half-hour train ride away on the LIRR. I decided to see what else was out there besides Rush and the other gay clubs I went to in the Chelsea area. I was starting to populate my Facebook friend list with prominent nightlife figures. My newsfeed was mostly party flyers that told me when and where, and I went. I was seduced by the glamor of Manhattan's downtown art and music scene, finding myself in clubs, bars, and every venue in between. With that, I discovered the world below Fourteenth Street: specifically, the Lower East Side.

I started to recognize the right people to know, the ones who had their own tables reserved, the ones who always had a flock of people orbiting them, but at the time I was still painfully shy and, in many ways, still felt like the same kid from middle and high school. Going up to these party hosts, glamour "it-girls," and downtown socialites and introducing myself was out of the question. I was never able to blend into the corner because I'm super tall and my affinity for high hair and loud outfits attracted people to me.

They wanted to know *who* I was, but *I* didn't even know who I was. I just knew that I belonged among these people, people who were unapologetic in their self-expression.

The ones I came across wrote for *Interview* Magazine (some of whom even helped launch it and were members of the iconic Warhol Factory), people who toured with legendary bands like Blondie and The Stooges, and people who knew just about *everybody*. What was I supposed to say? "HI, NICE TO MEET YOU. I'M AN UNDERAGE COLLEGE FRESHMAN WITH AN UNDECLARED MAJOR AND A PICTURE OF JOAN CUSACK'S HEADSHOT IN MY WALLET—WANNA SEE?"

I was nobody to these people.

I met Michael Musto, the legendary *Village Voice* journalist, who told me about some major article he was working on and then asked me what I did for a living. I was determined not to repeat my incident with my first college crush, Steve, by replying with some insipid non-sequitur, so I told him I was a dancer.

A DANCER.

I threw my back out Wet Swiffering once. Also, taking an elective on the history of dance freshman year does not qualify me to audition for a world tour anytime soon. Fearing that I would get caught in the lie I just blurted out, I told him I really liked the ascot tucked into his breast pocket and abruptly left to go bum a cigarette from someone outside. I thought it was better to flee the scene than have one of New York's most influential figures find out that I'm someone who, just the other night, torpedoed gravy into his mouth from a solo cup.

I wanted to fit in. I wanted to be just as cool as these people who breathed life into the downtown ethos. Instead of dealing with my social anxiety head on, I started adding these people as friends on Facebook. I decided that I would make my debut by getting noticed online, behind an avatar, first. Mind you, this was when Facebook was in its infancy. Many of these individuals hadn't already maxed out their friend lists and basically added anyone who looked like a downtown art freak, so I had no problem getting friend requests accepted.

I began communicating with these characters online, liking their posts and leaving comments, and they were starting to take notice of me, of my pictures in my usual exhi-bitionistic attire, and my absurd, ridiculous, and, oftentimes, raunchy humor. It was this approach to self-presentation on the internet that led to the night my real last name (which is indeed spelled Mania, but pronounced "Mahn-ya") became my official nickname, or stage name, if you will (also spelled Mania, but the way you pronounced it in your head when you saw the cover of this book.)

In 2009, there was only one band that mattered to me and that band was Semi Precious Weapons. They were head-lining a show at the Bowery Ballroom in the spring of 2010, and my friend Cecilia, whom I met on Twitter, and I decided to meet face-to-face for the first time by going to the show together.

We loaded up on booze at Cecilia's apartment on the Upper East Side and arrived downtown to the Bowery Ballroom shortly after. I knew many of the people I was shamelessly trying to get the attention of would be under the same roof because everyone was posting about it—this was *the* place to be that night.

My fake ID—somehow—got me in, even though at the age of eighteen, I still looked like the kid whose face is on the Farina box. You saw my prom picture. Cecilia and I walked downstairs to the bar area to have a drink. It was already crowded, but you could spot who the Lower East Side party-natives were versus who the young fans coming in from the tri-state area were. We grabbed our drinks and went upstairs, where the actual venue was. The stage was flanked by a pair of balconies, and there were also two other bar areas, one in the back of the room, and one directly above it on the second floor.

I immediately recognized some of the people I'd connected with on the internet. They stuck out, even among the hip, trendy crowd decked out in their flashiest going-out garb. It was like a spotlight followed them wherever they went. You were instantly curious; you wanted to know who they were, how they came to be. Did they always have that indefinable "it"?

My eyes fell on Darian Darling, a blonde bombshell exuding pure, unadulterated glamor (or glaMOUR, as she calls it), topped with a sequined beret, making everyone else in the room look like characters in a coloring book that have yet to be colored in. With a name inspired by Warhol Superstar Candy Darling, Darian, as her name denotes, was the darling of downtown Manhattan, always hosting the most chichi parties and events from the Hudson Hotel to The Box to The Standard—all staple venues in the nightlife community.

I made eye contact with Darian. When she gave me the you-look-familiar look, I knew there was no turning back. In my alcohol-fueled confidence, I went over and formally introduced myself. After exchanging a double-air kiss, she asked me, "Are you that Greg Mania from Facebook?", pronouncing "Mania" like anyone normally would. I was about to correct her on the pronunciation of my last name but instead of doing that, I confirmed that I was—without prefacing my answer with the, up until that night, faithful diction. We ended up exchanging numbers and she invited me to some of the upcoming parties she was scheduled to host, saying she would put me on her list. A list! Little did I know I would spend many nights of debauchery with her that often ended up with us texting each other the next morning and asking if we were alive. It was like hanging out with Patsy from the beloved British sitcom, *Absolutely Fabulous*.

I also found myself gravitating towards people with equally interesting monikers: Kenny Kenny, Miss Guy, Ladyfag, all of whom were present at the Bowery Ballroom that night. This was *the* place to be, remember? But there were two in particular that I also met that night, in addition to Darian, that became formative figures for me at the age of eighteen: Breedlove and Lady Starlight.

I'm always curious about the origin of someone's stage name/nickname/whatever you want to call it. I would come to learn that Lady Starlight had given Breedlove his name, back in 2003 when they were producing an event in the East Village at a bar called Rififi. The party was called "Freak Out!" and featured go-go dancing to psychedelic music and accompanying 1960s visuals. Breedlove, whose real name is Craig, needed a stage name, and Lady Starlight came across a shirt with the label that read, "Craig Breedlove for Sears." Craig Breedlove was a record-breaking race car driver with a clothing line at Sears in the 1960s, resulting in a moment of happenstance for the Breedlove I met in 2009. Lady Starlight adopted her name from the song "Lady Starlight" by The Sweet.

Darian was the one who introduced me to Breedlove and Starlight. They were curious to know more about me. I felt like I was talking to people I had known my entire life, people who already knew all my deep, dark secrets, my dreams, and saw something in me that I had yet to discover. They listened to me and I could see actual interest in their eyes, and a type of fire in them—one that held the nucleus of their very essence as people who were already icons, but didn't need fame or recognition to hold that title—and I knew that these were the people I wanted to surround myself with.

I'm fairly certain it wasn't memorable meeting me, seeing as I looked like just another young, barely legal kid dipping their toes into the downtown scene, but for me, meeting Breedlove and Lady Starlight in person, after following them closely on Myspace, was a moment when shifted something in me.

That night Bowery Ballroom would find itself hop-scotching from pop-cabaret to heavy metal to glam rock—all in the span of two hours.

Breedlove was the first to perform that night. He got on stage wearing a blue sweater with a rhinestone-encrusted red heart in the middle, followed by two backup dancers wearing spandex. He performed his infectious songs with the accompanying choreography, occasionally using a rotary phone and a mirror as props. The whole crowd couldn't help but fall for his undeniable charm, his cabaret-meets-disco-meets-pop melodies that made you want to clink your drink with a stranger's.

After Breedlove, Lady Starlight took to the stage and head-banged to Iron Maiden and chugged Jack Daniels. At the time, this was her act. It was a hybrid of performance art and heavy metal, which either had everyone shaking their heads in confusion or banging them along with her. I watched in awe, mostly because I wondered how much Icy Hot she uses in a year to alleviate any pain she may feel in her neck.

Then, it was finally time for Semi Precious Weapons to take the stage. Four men took to the stage, each donning clothing that directly correlated with their personality. Their lead singer, Justin, wore glittery gold pointed-toe heels, ripped tights with a repeated pattern of Marilyn Monroe's face, and black eyeliner so thick you would think he needed a jackhammer to take his makeup off at the end of the night, performed songs with lyrics that my eighteen-year-old self immediately wanted to get tattooed: "I can't pay my rent but I'm fucking gorgeous"; "put a diamond in it and bite down"; "I've been magnetic since I was a baby." I couldn't believe my eyes, my ears. I felt like a door had opened to reveal another version of myself, a version of myself that was becoming clearer to my view.

The energy of downtown Manhattan was palpable that night. The mantra of "filthy glamour"—a phrase coined by those in the Precious Empire—was at its peak and looking back I realize I literally watched history being made. The people I met that night, singing songs about dreaming so big that it makes life seem so boring, building Statues of Themselves, another favorite Semi Precious Weapons track of mine, came to do just that: they've gone on to open for the biggest pop stars in the world like Lady Gaga and Kesha, write chart-topping singles for artists like Justin Bieber, all while garnering fans from every corner of the world. It was at that moment that I realized I wanted to be a part of this history.

After the show, Justin Tranter approached our general vicinity. I'm terrible at guessing people's heights, so I'm going to say he's taller than me (I'm six-foot-four), but shorter than the Empire State Building (1,454-foot-three.) It's hard not to notice him, especially in the loud, excessively glamorous outfits he used to wear back then. It's also hard to register subject-verb agreement around him considering his aura and physical beauty render you speechless. If you haven't seen him or don't know what he looks like, I implore you to google him right now. I'll wait.

After talking to Darian and the rest of his motley crew, Justin's eyes landed on me. When I was introduced to him, I sounded like I had the verbal skill set of a drunk person trying to whisper a secret. He looked at me like he faintly recognized me and asked me, "Hey, are we friends on Facebook?" I thought, "Facebook? What's Facebook? You're pretty. Let's tongue-joust."

I probably didn't say anything for a good few seconds because as you well know by now, any third grader could definitely upstage my social skills. Then he asked me, "Aren't you that Mania kid?" I knew we were Facebook friends, but I definitely thought he was Too Cool to notice any of my posts, let alone pay attention to whatever malarkey I was going on about. For a second, I went mute. I didn't know how to react.

I regarded him as a deity—he did have a halo of blonde hair—and to hear my name in his mouth didn't feel real, but to hear it come out as the incorrectly pronounced version felt like finally getting that one Tetris piece that you needed.

I finally felt a sense of belonging come over me, a feeling that I never felt anywhere else: in grade school, in middle school, in high school, anywhere in New Jersey or even on a college campus. I gave myself a name that allowed me to be the most unbridled version of myself, even if it was a funny, ridiculous name—it was me and it was right there the whole time. Embracing the common mispronunciation of my name, and then deeming it my nickname, allowed myself the space to be me, unbridled from the reflex to dull or eradicate certain parts of myself in an effort to fit a mold that was impossible, for me, to fit in the first place.

My family still corrects people when they mispronounce our last name: receptionists at the doctor's office, restaurant servers who read the name on the credit card, and even telemarketers, but I haven't since that night. Don't get me wrong, sometimes I pronounce my name the traditional way when I introduce myself to someone—but that's only because I finally feel comfortable in my skin. I know that my name doesn't define me, rather I define it. And having that agency comes from embracing every part of me: the good, the bad, and everything in between. So, call me whatever you want, just don't spell my name "Gregg."

6. THE LANGUAGE OF NIGHTLIFE TRANSLATED

We'll stay in touch!
I'll add you on Facebook and occasionally "like" or comment on one of your posts but other than that, you won't hear from me until you see me out again in a month or so, which is when I'll promise you we'll stay in touch.

Hey!
I'm genuinely happy to see you!

Haaay!
I'm fucking **ADAMANT** about pushing the boundaries of my blood alcohol content tonight.

(In a questioning tone) Helllllllllllo?
Have we met?

I'm LIVING.
I'm aware of the fact that I'm a breathing, functioning, and

cognizant entity but don't care to look like it after the event photographer takes a decent photo of me LET'S RAGE.

I'm living for your look!
I'm a breathing, functioning, and cognizant entity whose sensory functions seem to heighten in response to your wardrobe choice this evening.

(A text received on the same day of each week) *Hey, what're you doing tonight?*
Come to my EVENT! There will be MUSIC! And GUESTS! BOOZE! W I N G E D E Y E L I N E R

Are you going to an after-hours party?
I am curious about the general trajectory of your night. Are you planning to engage in a modest amount of debauchery and POSSIBLY turn down for some things? OR do you plan to go to this questionable venue that doesn't even have a sign, make terrible decisions, and end up sitting on your landlord's face?

Can I charge my phone behind the bar?
Can I charge my phone behind the bar?

7. WHAT DO LINDSAY LOHAN, FORD MOTOR COMPANY, AND THE CONSTITUTION ALL HAVE IN COMMON?

They've all been in my hair!

Let me explain: I always felt invisible growing up. I was never popular because I was too busy getting called a fag and getting slammed into lockers; I wasn't nominated prom king; I wasn't considered to compete for Mr. LHS, which was an annual showcase my high school hosted every June where twelve seniors would perform in a talent show in an effort to win the coveted title of Mr. LHS and the crown that went with it. I was voted Most Likely to Cry in Every Bathroom at Best Buy Across the Country by my high school. But as you also now well know, I was the flamboyant theater kid. My desire to for attention and recognition was innate.

The first thing I learned about NYC nightlife is that everyone has a certain look. Darian is a blonde bombshell, dressing in the vein of blonde beauty icons from Marilyn Monroe to Farrah Fawcett to Madonna to Courtney Love, mixed with a little 1980s technicolor makeup palette, topped with, often times, a sequined beret. Breedlove, at the time, was going through an era where he solely wore bedazzled kaftans, accompanied by his long brown hair and signature pilot glasses. Justin always wore an ensemble that consisted of shimmery tights, sparkly pointed-toe heels, and a jacket adorned in grommets. My friend DJ VH1 (a.k.a. Brendan Sullivan) is always seen wearing a pair of white-rimmed sunglasses. You've seen him in Lady Gaga's music video for "Just Dance," you can't miss him.

I also learned that if you're trying to get noticed and make a name for yourself in a scene like this, repetition is important. You have to burn an image of yourself into people's brains so that you become memorable.

My thing? Hair. Very high hair. Hair that looks like it was combed with a grenade. Since it upstaged the Statue of Liberty in height (which, at the time, was inspired by 1980s NYC performance art icon John Sex), I decided to use it as a canvas for what some have affectionately dubbed as, "hair art," which were really just hair stencils. I thought they would complete the look I was going for, since all of the outfits I was already adorning myself in were the visual equivalent of a fog horn. The look I was going for was "one of the Von Trapp children who walked into CBGB and liked what he saw."

I thought: What better way to burn myself into people's memories than not only having an eleven-inch platinum mohawk, but taking it to the next level and featuring some sort of imagery in it? I was obsessed with the idea of elevating what it means to "sell your body" while making a critique of marketing and publicity strategies that have either become innovative, desperate, or attention-seeking. Personally, I chose to hone in on the attention-seeking element because well, I already have a billboard growing out of my head that has been the honorary recipient of many double-takes while walking down the street.

I had already seen people on Tumblr spray text and buzz cool images into their hair. I decided to put my own spin on this aesthetic. The first piece of art I featured in my hair was a stencil of Lindsay Lohan, and for a while I became known as "the kid with Lindsay Lohan in his hair."

Even on nights I didn't have anything or anyone sprayed into my hair, people would come up to me and check both sides of my mohawk for any images or portraits. I was doing something right; I was starting to have a certain look associated with me. *PMc* Magazine even wanted to interview me, and they even gave me creative control over the photos that would run with the interview. I asked my friend Ky to shoot my first magazine spread. I think the photo that ran with the piece accurately sums up my entire being best:

Photography by Ky Digregorio.

The "@" should basically be an option for me to select as a suffix when I'm filling out forms online. What better hair stencil to introduce myself to the world with in my first magazine write-up than the international symbol for HELLO LOOK AT ME AND GIVE ME ATTENTION.

Photo on the right courtesy of Nicky Digital.

Above is the Preamble accompanied with appropriate American flag imagery. Remember how I mentioned that my brother would often help me execute my projects? Well, he's the genius behind bringing all of these stencils to fruition. He meticulously cut each stencil using an X-Acto knife after I traced the images on translucent wax paper. He still has flashbacks to the time we did "We The People" because the font is so detailed that is scarred him for life. It took the longest out of all of them because cutting that grandiose-as-fuck "P" in "People" wasn't unlike he was performing open-heart surgery. I had to wipe the accumulating beads of sweat off of his forehead with a damp cloth when he was cutting that one out. Sometimes I think he jolts upright in the middle of the night because he has nightmares about this particular stencil.

I wish I had a deep, insightful response as to why I chose the Ford logo in my hair. I guess I've always been fascinated with product placement. I mean, look at music videos now—they're basically glorified commercials with fun outfits and theatrical lighting. I guess one can say this is one of my more Warhol-inspired hair pieces vis-à-vis the infamous Campbell's soup can pop art. Also it's, uh...social commentary!

Since I couldn't afford authentic Chanel, I decided to just spray the logo in my hair. Why spend the money on actual Chanel when you can exude the same display of wealth by spraying it on with ninety-nine-cent black hairspray from a Halloween store?! My favorite is the dude in the background who looks like if he were given three wishes, he would use all of them to make me disappear.

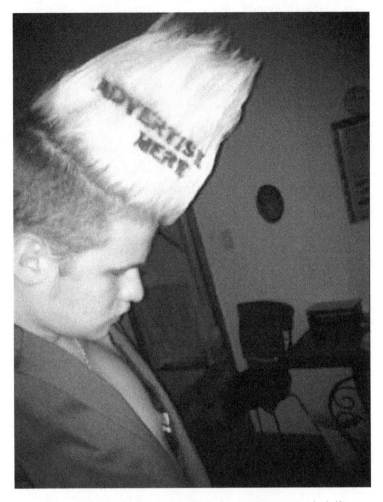

Seriously though, I will promote your product on my hair if the price is right. Please DM me to talk rates.

Using my altitudinous locks as a canvas proved to be successful in my attempt to make a name for myself in the nightlife world. I shared a little bit of the spotlight with some of the other club kids who never failed to provoke a "YAS!" with each look they sport and are frequently a source of inspiration—and sometimes blatant imitation—for and from a number of mainstream fashion houses and A-List pop stars and performers. I was finally gaining a sense of who I was and what I wanted to be: a unique amalgamation of comedy and outrageous fashion, forever inspired by my undying love for people like Phyllis Diller and Joan Rivers.

Once I had a look and started sporting it on the regular, I was getting attention from photographers and blogs like the mega-popular blog *Humans of New York*. Brandon Stanton, the photographer and genius behind the Facebook page, photographed me the first time in SoHo during his project's infancy. I got emails from agencies for various projects, one of them for a punk-inspired *Vogue* spread, which I didn't end up getting because well, I have the elegance and grace of a newborn deer. Plus, I'm just not model material; I've eaten at Wendy's twice in one day.

Using my hair as a canvas put a foot in the door that allowed a sliver of validation to slip in. It was a major stepping stone for me because the way I was dressing myself, styling my hair, and leaving the house looking like I was brought to life from a graphic novel—letting myself look like the person I wanted to be—gave me the confidence to pursue the person I wanted to become: a writer. Sculpting my hair made me want to say more and be more myself, on a canvas that couldn't be erased by shampoo.

8. IT'S JUST ANOTHER MAGIC MONDAY

Like school, my night life also followed a schedule. There was something going on every night of the week, except on weekends because those nights were reserved for those coming in for a night out from the surrounding areas. Historically, this group of people has been dubbed as the "bridge-and-tunnel" crowd, meaning those who travel into Manhattan from New Jersey, Connecticut, Long Island, and, depending on whom you ask and what they consider bridge-and-tunnel, Staten Island and the outer boroughs. This phrase is widely considered a pejorative because this crowd has been perceived as "unsophisticated" and "has probably gotten alcohol poisoning at Applebee's before." Now, I'm not a fan of making a sweeping generalization, so I'm not saying *all* of these people fall into the categories listed above, but, in my experience, trying to go out in the Lower East Side on a Saturday night and dodging projectile vomit that is composed of ninety percent Four Loko and an occasional homophobic slur from a dude in an Adelphi hoodie has been something me and my friends have learned to actively avoid, even though I geographically qualify as bridge-and-tunnel. But I kept my nightlife schedule of Monday through Thursday, using the weekends to recharge.

On Wednesdays, you would find me at Delancey and Ludlow, nicknamed the DL, where my friends who worked at Patricia Field would host a party on the third floor, surrounded by palms and a giant fountain in the middle of the dancefloor. The Zand Collective, which is comprised of avant-garde goths led by nightlife power couple Kayvon and Anna Zand, hosted a party on the floor below. I'd have a few drinks at the DL, and then sometimes swing by The Box on Chyrstie Street, just a few blocks away, to visit Darian, who would go on to host there on Wednesday nights for a few years. I love The Box because they always have performances that are the reason NYC nightlife is famous; you haven't lived until you've seen a burlesque dancer spray the crowd with champagne from her cooch. On Thursdays, there was POGO, another weekly party hosted by Darian and a few of our other friends in the basement of Hotel Chantelle on Ludlow Street. There was another party, upstairs, called Generation Wild, for the metal heads, so it was perfect for someone like me who needed to take a break from getting saucy to Beyoncé in the basement and go rage to Motley Crüe upstairs. But, there's only one party that, despite how inebriated I was at it every week, still remains crystal clear in my memory.

Magic Monday was Breedlove's weekly party where he would perform his unique blend of pop-cabaret-disco songs on top of the bar at St. Jerome, a now-defunct dive bar on Rivington Street in the Lower East Side. He would always have a bill of other local bands and artists perform that night, too, so it was a great opportunity to get a taste of the local music scene. It wasn't totally unlike Studio 54, in a sense that it was the same type of crowd you would see gathering at a designated spot reserved for your debauchery and accompanying antics.

The first Magic Monday was held at St. Jerome back in the summer of 2010, just a few months after Semi Precious Weapons headlined at Bowery Ballroom. I saw Breedlove post the flyer for it on Facebook. Even though I was eighteen, I knew I had to find myself at that bar, on that night. I grabbed some friends and we made our way to the Lower East Side, and luckily, I didn't have any trouble getting in because, at the time, the bouncer didn't really check IDs, and by that, I mean there wasn't even a bouncer.

The first thing I remember upon entering St. Jerome was how fucking hot it was. I remember seeing an A/C but I'm pretty sure it was just "for display." It was already fucking crowded and everyone was sweaty, and every surface of that bar was sticky due to alcohol or god knows what else. It was also the size of a fucking bento box, which made it even hotter. We were basically drinking inside of a rotisserie. It was small, dark, and hot.

It was perfect.

I immediately recognized people like Darian, Justin Tranter, Lady Starlight, and, of course, Breedlove. I also saw a bunch of other faces, many of which were slabbed in glitter and immaculately applied eyeliner, and they became the same faces I would see every Monday night for almost four years. I've never seen so many wigs: pink bobs, long blue ones with bangs, a yellow perm. My friend, Laura Desiree, a burlesque performer from Toronto, introduced me to her wig, whom she named Dallas. I felt really underdressed compared to everyone else. I was wearing baby-blue jeans and a graphic T-shirt—not even ONE hole in my jeans or even a fun pair of socks. Who the fuck was I? I started to feel (more) anxious just standing there and gawking, so I bought a Bud and squeezed into a (very sticky) booth.

Then a fog machine was turned on.

A sequin-clad Breedlove, who was wearing the very same blue sweater with a red rhinestone-encrusted heart I saw him wear a few months earlier at Bowery Ballroom, holding a rotary phone in one hand and a microphone in the other, uttered his now-signature line: *you can press play.*

The music started and he sang his song, "Love on the Telephone," while two dancers, Kelsey and Leigh, performed the accompanying choreography. He then went onto to perform his other songs, "Oh, Pierre," (my personal favorite), "Me and the Boys," "OK By Me," and "New York City Rooftop," which we filmed the music video for two years later.

The minute Breedlove started performing I forgot about the amount of sweat permeating from my pores and became completely transfixed by the scene that was unfolding around me. There was a palpable feeling that night, a feeling that something like this would never happen again. I don't think I'm the only one who felt that way.

My friend Ky felt it, too, because she turned the photos she spent her time taking over the years at Magic Monday into a book called *American Nights.* The entire book consists of photographs Ky has taken of our Magic Monday family throughout the several Lower East Side bars that have served as Magic Monday's home over the years. This book is basically my generation's version of the iconic CBGB & OMFUG photo book. Here's a glimpse of what our nights looked like:

Allison Harvard & friend

Penny Lane

Breedlove

Chew Fu

Club Ali and Leah Pinero

Darian Darling

Joce

Ky

Cole Whittle

Kat Llyod

Yours Truly

Mike Greco and MaryAnne Piccolo

Timothe Victor

Lady Starlight

All photos courtesy of Ky Digregorio.

As you can tell from the photos, this weekly cult-like party attracted crowds of vibrant, magnetic individuals that I befriended. Each week, we would reunite under the same roof to dance and sing along to Breedlove's lyrics that we'll know by heart to the grave.

From the first night, Magic Monday had this familiar sense of family, like these were people I've known my whole life and that night was just a missing piece of the puzzle I was trying to find in the scheme of trying to find where I belong. When I went to my senior prom, I don't think I even danced to one song. I felt welcome in this tiny rectangular box of a bar.

Before I was clueless about basically everything: my identity, where I fit in, and where the fuck the cars driving in deserts in car commercials are going. But now I was eighteen and saw a possible trajectory. I didn't know the destination, but I didn't care, because at least I had a path to follow, and that's all because I found myself in a community filled with people exactly like me: people who didn't know who they were or where they were going until they came to New York and found each other.

After that night, who I was and who I was meant to be became clearer. I felt charged. They shot the pistol that made me take off like a runner at the starting line.

Every Monday I made sure to dress the fuck up: high hair, shoes that guaranteed orthopedic insoles in my future. There's something life-affirming about coming into a room of people who will praise and bow down and tell you they love your look, no matter what you're wearing. You can be in full drag or wearing a cool band tee with a bandana and at least four people will come up to you and tell you they're "living" for you—because all they cared about was your company.

Your presence mattered to them. If I was absent one Monday night, I'd get a cluster of texts from different people, asking me where I was. The party—and more importantly, its people —molded me into the person I am today.

Lady Starlight would regale me with stories about how, when she was on tour anywhere that wasn't New York—or sometimes, it was in New York, just not performing for her usual crowd (read as: us, her friends)—people would *stare* at her, reactionless, baffled at this woman on stage wearing something akin to a period piece, spinning heavy metal on vinyl, and occasionally stepping in front of her turntables to dance with a set of pom-poms and then, in the blink of an eye, chug from a bottle of Jack Daniels. It wasn't even a few years ago when Starlight joined Gaga on stage at Lolla-palooza during the middle of her set to set cans of hairspray of fire to "Metal Militia" by Metallica, an act they used to perform together all the time before Gaga left New York to pursue a career that would eventually unfold before the entire world. Even then, at Lollapalooza, people didn't know how to react.

I remember watching Starlight open for Gaga a few times, and each time I couldn't gauge the audience's reac-tions. Some just didn't get it; some thought it was some sort of comedic bit; some were drunk and just didn't care and went along with it. I thought if Lady Starlight, this woman who's totally badass and doesn't give one singular shit about her audience staring at her with a mix of puzzlement, bemuse-ment, and perhaps fear, and instead finds the humor in it and the fuel to keep doing it, then I can, too. I went on to adopt the same mentality in my writing: if I'm having fun writing it, someone will have fun reading it.

Magic Monday continued every Monday night for a few years until we said goodbye to it along with St. Jerome, which is now a juice bar or Bank of America, or whatever the fuck they're replacing every bar with character and history in NYC with these days. It was something about that particular duration of time that made it seem like the "Golden Age" of New York, which is funny because the original so-called "Golden Age" of downtown Manhattan in the 1970s is what drew most of us to NYC in the first place. There are so many parties and events in NYC every night of the week, but so many of these events are about who you know, what list you're on, and how many followers you have on Instagram.

The "magic" in Magic Monday came from its authenticity. It was all about the music, the fashion, cheap beer, shiny disco balls, fake hair, fake nails and mostly importantly, each other—we went to indulge in a space and time to let loose, dance, drink, have fun, ask each other about our dreams, our goals, mend our broken hearts, or watch new love flourish— we were there for each other, physically and emotionally. I get nostalgic thinking about it because although many of us still meander downtown to the same joints, many of us have also moved to different parts of the country or have continued onto another path in life.

I'm not sure the words on these pages will ever accurately describe this period of my life, but I hope at least, for you, dear reader, that you find, or realize you will find, a community of people who encourage you to take the mask you wear off and embrace the things about you that you think are too weird or too odd. There's a group of people out there who will welcome you with open arms because the only thing they're interested in is your company, your spirit. And for those of you reading this who spent those nights with me dancing, singing, drinking, smoking, and making out, the only appropriate thing I can say to you is a quote from one of my favorite Breedlove lyrics: "I can't believe how much I love you."

9. CASUAL GO-GO

Magic Monday went on hiatus for a few weeks because Breedlove went to open for Lady Gaga on her Born This Way Ball tour, so that left me and my friends with nothing to do on Monday nights. Our whole routine was uprooted. What were we supposed to do, laundry? Watch *Bones*?!

After the release of *American Nights*, Ky started to DJ in between Breedlove's sets on Monday nights, so she looked for another place to DJ on Monday nights while Breedlove went on tour. She got a shift at a burlesque bar in the Lower East Side called Nurse Bettie. Our friend, Danielle, who was one of the bartenders for the second half of the Magic Monday era, picked up a bartending shift on the same night, at the same bar.

On our first Magic Monday-less Monday night, I helped Ky bring her vinyl records to Nurse Bettie and sat next to her while I sipped a whiskey ginger. After a few (read as: too many) drinks, I found myself on the stage where the burlesque dancers perform their acts on the weekend and started go-go dancing to David Bowie's "Young Americans."

I was wearing obscenely distressed black denim short-shorts, a white tank-top, and a black wide-brimmed hat in the style of Boy George, so it went nicely with the vibe we had going on. Danielle loved what I was doing so she turned on the little red-hued stage light that hung above the stage, and I continued dancing well into the night/early morning. Ky made a joke about how I was casually go-go dancing in the corner and our communal lightbulb went off and alas, "Casual Go-Go" was, well, a go(go).

"Dollhouse," a weekly event featuring a female bartender, female DJ spinning 50s, 60s, punk rock, garage, glam, disco, and funk, and a flamboyant male go-go dancer, was born. We thought it would be fun to reassign outdated gender roles with a female-lead DJ-bartender combo and a theatrical go-go dancer whose act leaned more towards the realm of performance art.

I was trying to channel Lady Starlight more than what one would associate with traditional go-go dancers. Our party quickly turned into the place to be. Not only did we serve as the substitute home for the Magic Monday crowd, we also welcomed a number of newcomers. This bona fide burlesque bar in the Lower East Side transformed into an environment that embraced the unconventional; no one was doing what we were doing. We were like a yurt on Airbnb.

My go-go routine, which started as a joke, turned into something I actually prepared for every week. I would watch clips on YouTube of people like Dita Von Teese and Bob Fosse and try to mimic their movements and incorporate them into choreography that could fit the genre of music that Ky was DJing. At first, I was nervous, especially considering I hadn't been on stage (or a platform, for that matter) since I Rickrolled audiences in high school. So, in order to alleviate my nerves, I just imagined everyone in the bar wearing nothing but Julia Roberts' wig from *Mother's Day*.

I was no Hell's Kitchen (one of Manhattan's prominent gayborhoods) go-go dancer; I didn't don a jockstrap nor a harness. If you go to a gay club in Hell's Kitchen, you'll see go-go dancers who are so built you could drive a Toyota Highlander into their rock-hard abs and the airbags would deploy. But the reaction I was trying to illicit wasn't about giving someone a boner as much as it was to be a spectacle. I wanted to be a centerpiece.

I would arrive at Bettie's around ten to have a drink and do some homework at the bar that was due the following day, because I'm a serious academic. Showtime was at midnight; I had two hours to get my work done and get buzzed enough to up there and do my thing. For the most part, the crowd consisted of the usual suspects—friends roaming the Lower East Side—but sometimes, we'd get strait-laced-Wall Street-looking types looking to have a martini after a long day of shouting about hedge funds into their Bluetooths before going home to watch Bloomberg TV.

These guys would meander in on a Monday night and end up seeing this:

They were usually the ones who were first to leave, which was fine because we didn't really care to mingle with a bunch of guys who consider their affinity for IPAs a personality trait. Also, the best thing about being a go-go dancer? YOU DON'T HAVE TO TALK TO ANYONE.

Here's the thing: I have, and I shit you not, TERRIBLE HEARING. I'm going to need Miracle Ear by the time I'm thirty. When I was little, I would listen to music so loudly through headphones that it permanently damaged my hearing. Seriously. When my roommates use the TV after me, they look like that famous poster of that dude being blown away by his TV set because I've been watching *Law and Order: SVU* at fucking volume level ninety-eight *with* closed captioning. And it didn't help that I was surrounded by reverberating club music multiple nights a week. I *never* know what anyone is saying to me at the club; I always just nod and say "cool!" to everything. My friend Gina refuses to go anywhere with me that isn't a library because she's sick of repeating herself three-thousand fucking times because I can't hear what she's saying to me whenever we're at a bar or a club.

Also, I hate hosting. I could never be an actual promoter. A lot of people in nightlife make their living this way: they work at night, sleep all day, and do it all over again. I, on the other hand, was a student by day, so having this type of schedule, as many night-lifers do, was out of the question if I was ever going to go to class and get the degree I was hemorrhaging money for. Also, I CAN'T HEAR YOU, EVER.

So, go-go dancing it was. Because not only did I have to talk to anyone and pretend that I could catch a single fucking word of what they were saying to me, I also got tipped. Granted, I was tipped mostly by friends. When Breedlove came home, he stopped by Nurse Bettie one Monday night and taught me to slip some dollar bills under my garter, tights, or whatever ridiculous piece of clothing I was performing in before I would even go on stage. He learned this from Lady Starlight, and he passed this wisdom down onto me: slipping a few of your own bills into your clothing will incline people to tip if they see some cash hanging somewhere on your person already.

I didn't make a ton of money, but I made enough to cover minor expenses and maybe buy a bite to eat from the McDonald's across the street after, which, for a student budget, is like winning the Powerball.

We found a routine, again, every Monday night. It was glamorous, and it was all ours. Our little space on Norfolk Street was our new home. Now, whenever a song like "Heart of Glass," "Young Americans," "I Want You to Want Me," or "I Hate Myself For Loving You" comes on when I'm listening to music, I'm instantly transported back to spring 2013 and the faces I would see from my platform flash before my eyes like a reel. I'd be in my own little world, above everyone, watching all my friends make out, laugh, cry, and drink until they couldn't see straight anymore. I knew those days wouldn't last forever, but sometimes I wish they did. When I tell people I used to go-go dance, they'd sometimes ask if I'd ever do it again. I say if I didn't have a bedtime at eight and wasn't prone to pulling a muscle just by coughing, I would. But I had fun while it lasted.

I performed my last casual go-go routine in May of 2013 when I graduated from Hofstra. I moved back to New Jersey to live with my parents and decided to celebrate graduation by performing a strip tease with my graduation gown as my final go-go routine. "Dollhouse" would soon leave its location on Norfolk Street and would marry itself to Magic Monday now that Breedlove was back in town again.

The summer after graduation I got an internship at *CREEM* Magazine. My first piece was with an interview with an up-and-coming singer-songwriter, my first by-line in print shortly to follow. I also developed an interest in pursuing comedy writing, professionally. I had options, and opportunities, and it was up to me to figure out which path to follow. But just because I wanted to, doesn't mean I knew how to. Before I could take the next step, I found myself in a situation where I would have to get myself back on my feet, first.

10. ROY

I was apprehensive about including this chapter in the first place, because this is supposed to be a zany book filled with ridiculous jokes and stories about me being uncouth and reconciling myself with the fact that I used to be someone who unironically wore a bullet belt from Hot Topic. But I realized I couldn't write a memoir about going from the world of nightlife to writing and comedy without acknowledging the catalyst that caused me to shift my trajectory: my relationship with someone whom I'll call Roy.

Before Roy, I went from someone who shamelessly friended people online to someone accepting friend requests from total strangers. It didn't irk me that I was getting a ton of friend requests from strangers, mostly because by the end of fall 2012 and into spring 2013, I was in peak nightlife mode. I was getting tagged and mentioned in a lot of the party photos that would circulate on Facebook and social pages like Nicky Digital and Guest of a Guest.

My blog also saw an exponential increase in traffic because my writing was picking up momentum and started to become popular on Facebook. I wasn't surprised strangers were connecting and interacting with me; my profiles were all public. Also, I used to be that stranger, trying to make friends on the internet. By that spring, I was accepting friend requests from teens in Oklahoma to club kids in London. One of those people whose friend request I accepted was Roy's.

I usually didn't spend too much time investigating who was requesting to be my friend online, and if I did, it was usually because I thought their style was remarkable or thought they were cute, both of which happened to be the case with Roy. He looked like someone from a boy band, as in you might have taped pictures of him in your locker or above your bed in high school. He had flowy brown hair and a smile that would immediately get him cast in an Abercrombie & Fitch campaign. I immediately had a crush on him.

Shortly after becoming Facebook friends with him, he started liking almost every single one of my status updates and photos. I noticed, of course, and was like, IS THIS DATING? I did some light snooping (going through every one of his photos dating back to 2008) and discovered that he had a boyfriend. Fuck. After convincing myself not to put my head in the microwave, I tried to put him out of sight, out of mind. He had a boyfriend and lived in the middle of Pennsylvania, so it wasn't going to happen! But he kept liking my photos, posts, and leaving a comment every once and a while, which made pretending he didn't exist difficult.

About a month or two before my college graduation, he messaged me on Facebook to tell me that he found me awe-inspiring, loved how I chose to express myself through my personal style, and would be honored if I could introduce him to the world of NYC nightlife come fall. He got accepted to the Pratt Institute and would be moving to Brooklyn to study interior design. I was flattered, and excited that he would basically be right next door. We exchanged phone numbers, and I told him I was excited to hang out in August. I checked my phone obsessively throughout the day, not paying attention in class, waiting for him to text me first. Occasionally, I'd chastise myself for getting my hopes it because: 1. I didn't know if he was actually into me, and 2. he had a boyfriend. Until he didn't.

I noticed that he wasn't posting about his boyfriend, the pictures of them together suddenly ceasing, until it became apparent that they broke up when I saw his relationship status change to "single." I felt bad for approximately 0.24 seconds and then proceeded to do a little jump for joy because I'M TRASH. But even if he was newly single, I didn't think he could be into someone like me.

Could he?

I think I'm cute—if you squint—but I didn't even know if I was his type. It was the typical case of the "he can have anyone he wants, why would he go for me?" thought pattern I used to maintain as a canned response to any dude who expressed interest in me because of my severely fluctuating self-esteem and confidence at the time.

And then he texted me. It was the summer of 2013. I had just graduated and moved back in with my parents. I was still driving the Honda Civic my brother, Andy, let me borrow since he wasn't using it. He took the train to his job at Newark Liberty International Airport, so in the meantime I had a car and the freedom that came with it. I would drive up to the city every few days to hit up a party or hang out with Ky and our friends in Bushwick. I didn't have a job—I wasn't even looking for one—because I was still tethered to the lifestyle I had in college, the one I spent oscillating between two different worlds. Except one world was no more: I wasn't in school anymore. Trying to retain some sense of familiarity, I continued my charades around the city even though I didn't live as close anymore.

Roy and I started texting each other every day that summer. He was excited to begin school at Pratt and to finally hang out with me in the city. I was excited, too, because I was slowly convincing myself that he was into me, especially with his texts becoming progressively flirtier. He would also send me pictures—not those kind—just selfies. Listen, I'm an idiot. I don't actually know if someone likes me *like that* unless they write it on a brick and throw it through my bedroom window, but even I could tell that he was flirting with me. My crush on him escalated.

I made plans to go to a comedy show on the Upper East Side with some friends at the end of August that summer. I drove up to the city that night because it was summer and few things are as idyllic as driving through Manhattan, chain-smoking and listening to The Undertones. The thought of smoking a cigarette now churns my stomach. So does driving in Manhattan. But I was twenty-two and romanticized the soft glow of a traffic light hitting my face while puffing on a Marlboro Red because I was a Sad Tumblr Gay™ who listened to "Blue Jeans" by Lana Del Rey one too many times.

I avoided the nightmare of parking by parking my car somewhere in the Lower East Side. I took a train uptown to meet my friends for the show. I spent the entire show, fidgety and antsy, because I knew Roy was moving into his dorm that day and I was dying for him to text me. Sure enough, right as the comedy show was ending, I get a text from Roy asking me if I wanted to get a drink. Disregarding any unspoken rules of waiting X amount of time to respond to a text, I immediately responded with a resounding, "DUH."

Since he was underage, I knew which bar to take him to. It's the same place that I've been going to since being underage myself, plus I knew all the bartenders, so I knew we wouldn't run into any issues. I said goodnight to my friends and told him to meet me in the Lower East Side. Since he didn't know his way around yet, I told him he could hop on the F train just a few blocks away from his campus.

It was an insufferably humid night, one of those nights when it feels like summer had no plans to loosen her sweaty grip on the city anytime soon. I was ostensibly nervous, so after I got off the train at Delancey Street, I ducked into Welcome to the Johnsons, a dive right around the corner, to gulp down a shot to calm my nerves. I figured I could pop out when he got to the area.

Fifteen minutes and two shots later, he called me to tell me he got off the train. I told him to meet me in front of the McDonald's on Delancey Street, near where the F train would spit him out at the Delancey/Essex Street station. I didn't see him emerge from the subway—there's approximately 89,000 exits and entrances at that particular subway station—and when I finally did lay eyes on him, he was illuminated by the giant golden arches.

He saw me and grinned.

My heart was beating so fast I thought it was going to fracture a rib. Normally, the golden arches of McDonald's have an effect on me not unlike the Greek Sirens, whose seductive calls lead sailors to their imminent deaths. Even if I'm not hungry, I can usually find something on the menu that I'm in the mood for. But that night I was bewitched by the Adonis approaching me.

We embraced like we had known each other for a lifetime. It wasn't even awkward at all, which I thought it was going to be because, well, I've met me. After exchanging pleasantries, I proposed grabbing a drink at the bar that would quickly become our spot.

We didn't go on a *real* date until about a month later. I was too shy to make the first move, so I waited for him to. I was convinced he liked me in the way I liked him, I could tell just by how he looked at me. It was palpable. But of course, YA BOY WASN'T ABOUT TO DO ANYTHING ABOUT IT OTHER THAN REMAIN MUTE FOR AN ETERNITY.

But later that night, he kissed me for the first time under the covers of his twin-sized bed.

Things escalated, physically, from there.

I started staying the night, leaving in the morning to go pick up my car which was still parked in the Lower East Side to drive home to New Jersey. It became our weekly routine, until I decided to break it by asking him if he wanted to go on a date. I didn't know what he was looking for, if we were just fooling around or what, but once he agreed to the date, I was thrilled.

I'd been burned by love before, sure, but this time I let myself embrace whatever story we were telling. I felt safe with him, like there was a sense of security I've never known but innately trusted.

I picked this swank hole-in-the-wall vegetarian spot on Orchard Street. I met up with Roy on Delancey so we could walk to the restaurant together. He was wearing a pair of clear, aviator glasses, and a giant, wraparound shawl that communicated to anyone that he had a comprehensive knowledge of probiotics. The comedian in me was overcome with the urge to start firing bits off into my iPhone: *Where are we going on our date, the Vitamin Shoppe?* But I loved it. I thought, "only my guy," and hoped he was thinking the same thing when he saw me in my red and black leopard-print skinny jeans from Trash & Vaudeville.

After getting seated and ordering a bottle of wine that I'm pretty sure I'm still paying off, we placed an order for two kale salads. I have a natural aversion to any place that doesn't have a kids' menu so I'll give you one guess as to which one of us pretended to actually like their kale salad. I didn't want him to be turned off by my unironic love of chain restaurants, so I decided to finish the salad I would have, in any other instance, immediately substituted with sweet potato fries or onion rings. After we finished our meals—I was still hungry because the salad was like four pieces of oven-roasted kale and JESUS BE A NUMBER SIX WITH A LARGE FRY— we made our way to what would become our bar.

It would be our first and last date, but not for a lack of chemistry, something we had in abundance, or commitment, something I was sure we would figure out, or so I thought.

We'd continue meeting up at the bar and heading back to his place after for the next few months. I started to wish we could skip the part where we'd drink ourselves into oblivion, but a part of me was scared that whatever we had going on, this undefined thing—and it's not like I believed he was scared of labeling it, he did say yes to a date after all!—what we felt for each other, would extinguish if we broke this custom. It'd crack if I even proposed doing something else like going to a movie or doing something during the—God forbid—daytime. It started to feel like something delicate that even the slightest shift could destroy, or worse, break the illusion I was subconsciously feeding into, blissfully ignorant of.

By this time, I knew that I loved him. I knew it deeply, unequivocally. I couldn't take the ambiguity of whatever we had going on between us. I texted him asking him if I could come over one night, just so we could hang out and talk. I thought if I made my desires known, then maybe the uncertainty would dissipate and we could build and nurture a healthy relationship based on mutual understanding.

By the time December rolled around, finals were around the corner for him. It was time for that end-of-semester hustle—I knew it well—so we weren't going out as much. Instead of meeting at our spot one night, I drove up to Brooklyn and parked right next to the bodega we'd usually stop in to buy a few beers from before heading back to his dorm. I told him that I needed to talk to him, that it wouldn't take long. He took a break from his final projects to meet me outside.

It was cold and a light rain, mist-like, started to fall. We sat on a bench outside his dorm and I spilled my guts: I told him that I loved him, and that even though we didn't define what our relationship was, I wanted him to know about everything that was simmering under the surface. I looked him right in the eye as I said all of this, to let him know I meant every word. I didn't know where this confidence and ability to make eye contact for more than four seconds came from, but I attributed it to the authenticity of my feelings for him.

After I told him what I had definitely rehearsed for the entire hour it took me to drive up to Brooklyn, he looked away and didn't say anything for what seemed like a few good minutes. He didn't say I love you back and we ended up talking for two hours, but those two hours are a blur in my mind. I couldn't really make sense of what he was saying. Even as he was saying it, I couldn't fully grasp what he meant. It didn't make any sense, now or back then. Even as I write this, it feels fragmented, each piece unable to fit with any of the others I have spread out in front of me. An unsolvable puzzle.

It felt like someone had replaced the Roy I knew with this decoy that speaks in out-of-context Marina Abramović quotes. I remember him repeating the phrase "wishy-washy," and that he wanted to "pause this" until he "figured out the essence of things."

I was too bewildered to respond. I was shocked, because the entire time we've known each other, I thought we were on the same page; I was confident that I would go home that night with someone I could start introducing as my boyfriend instead of a friend who sees me naked all the time. He'd explicitly told me, twice, that he had feelings for me, but when he told me that night that he wasn't sure if he had feelings for me after all, I asked him to clarify: did he mean right now, or ever? He said he didn't know how he felt about anything, but that he did want to keep seeing me. I asked him what he meant by that, and he said he didn't know. I left that night more confused than heartbroken.

That night would be the last time I saw Roy, but it wouldn't be the end of his presence in my life. He would dodge any invitation to hang out after that, and when the holidays came around, two weeks later, he apologized for being busy and made a vague promise to hang out once he was back on campus after the holidays. We had gone from talking every day to barely talking at all, only exchanging a few texts here and there. His posts on Facebook were all over the place, sometimes joyful and other times dark and morose. I couldn't make sense of him or anything anymore. He would go from tender to aggressive and back to tender again with me, and when I would try to get him to open up, he only closed himself up more.

One night I reminded him that I was there for him, and he responded with a terse "fuck you."

I didn't know what I had done. I asked him if I had done something to upset him, and when he didn't respond, I sent him a string of apologies for whatever it was that I could have done to warrant such an angry response. A few days later, he texted me as if nothing had happened. I decided to drop it because he seemed to be in better spirits.

I knew that, in the early stages of our relationship, or whatever you want to call it, he had a drug problem as a teen. I knew that he was prone to self-destructive behavior. I've gone down the path of self-destruction, too, and I also had my share of dark times when I had to be reeled in—I was, however, never really that much of a drug user, even weed makes me anxious and paranoid—but I foolishly believed that this time would be different, that we would be each other's antidote. I started to piece together the moments that I didn't think anything of, let slip because it wasn't something that I myself didn't do: casual use of Adderall to finish up a project, a downer to unwind.

I didn't think anything of it until one night he popped a Vyvanse, which is a stimulant that treats ADHD, at the bar. It's not like I've never met an addict—I've had a number of friends who struggled with addiction—but I never dated, nor grown close enough to notice the almost-inconspicuous behavior that, more times than not, can open a door that should remain closed. I remember asking him why he took it, was he going to the library after this to finish a paper or what? He mentioned that it was just leftover Vyvanse a friend gave him, and I dropped it. I didn't realize he was starting down the path of relapse.

I didn't hear much from Roy over the holidays. I was miserable and confused. When he finally did come back to campus, it wasn't for long. He eventually ended up getting kicked out of Pratt a few weeks into the spring semester. My only source of information was his friend, Hannah, whom I've gotten close to over the course of knowing Roy. Hannah told me that he was found in possession of drugs and was immediately kicked out of Pratt. He could be considered for readmission if he sought the appropriate help. I wasn't clear on the details, but it was apparent that he was using again.

He moved back home to Pennsylvania after getting kicked out. I barely heard from him. He would either respond to my texts with something cryptic at five in the morning or not respond at all. I remained in contact with Hannah the entire time, just so I could feel a sense of proximity, a way to be there for him from afar. She informed me that his mother eventually kicked him out, and that he was living with a friend in town. To say I was worried would be an undeniable understatement. In a panic, I reached out to his brother, Mark, who told me that their mom kicked him out because his path of self-destruction was wreaking havoc on the house and their family. They were hoping Roy would get arrested because at least he'd be able to detox in a jail cell.

It was a cold March morning when Hannah called me in hysterics. Roy had sent her a Facebook message that sounded very final, very real. I panicked. I didn't know what to do, but I had to do something. I called the local police in his town and told them that I thought my friend was in trouble, that, according to the message he sent Hannah that morning, he might have swallowed a bunch of pills. I couldn't give them an address of where he was, only that of his parents' house, which was useless since they kicked him out. The police said they couldn't do anything unless I knew where he was. I felt completely helpless. And even if I wanted to get in my car and drive there, it would take me no fewer than two hours to get there. Even still, I didn't know where he was. I knew he was still in his hometown; I just didn't know where or with whom.

I was able to track down the friend he was staying with by going through his recent Facebook posts to see if there was someone or somewhere tagged recently. I messaged her and she, thankfully, responded immediately. She was at work, but said that she would send her mom, who was home, to go check on him. She found him asleep. He was fine. He didn't take anything, or if he did, it wasn't enough to do the deed.

He updated his Facebook status a few hours later with something innocuous, and didn't even offer an explanation to anyone regarding the message that sent Hannah, us, into a panic. He never spoke a word of it.

This wouldn't be the last time something like this happened, and the outcome was almost always the same: he would allude to the fact that he would harm himself in some way, but wouldn't go through with it, wouldn't even speak a word about it or acknowledge the fear and pain he was inciting in those around him who loved him. He once sent me a picture, with no accompanying text or explanation, just a picture, of his slashed wrists at four in the morning, and when I woke up, I called and texted him until he answered. When he eventually answered, he said he was fine in a tonality as though he had just scraped his knee.

I started to understand why his own family turned their backs on him, why they did what they did when they kicked him out. There are only so many times someone can drag you into the abysmal hopelessness of their mind until you start to feel like you're losing yours. There's only so much you can take. You do everything you can to save them from themselves only to realize you've gone out so far, you can't see land anymore. I didn't realize how far out I was until that spring.

I was extremely depressed to the point where I feared that I'd succumb to my dark thoughts, the whispers that began to haunt me. I was losing control: my mind felt like it was slipping, forfeiting its own agency just so I wouldn't have to feel this way anymore. As a result, I started cutting, to regain a sense of control. It was a temporary relief from the pain I was already in, a new pain to distract myself with. Then one day I just broke.

I remember that day, specifically. It was Easter. It was a beautiful spring day, and my family and I were preparing the house for Easter dinner. My mom tasked me with decorating the house with flowers from the garden, but the whole day felt impossible to live through. Everything I did, every movement I made, felt attached to one-thousand-pound weights. My mind wouldn't stop racing. I was never more scared of myself, my mind, the thoughts that permeated from within, but felt like were coming from an external source, a source born from a breach in reality.

I couldn't take it anymore; I wanted to rip my skin off. I would bang my head against the wall or hit myself, just to jolt myself from the mental quicksand I was in. I've lived with depression since being a young teen, but this time felt different. I needed help; Roy and I both did. By April, Roy ended up in rehab. His friend that he had been staying with eventually convinced him to go, and he checked into a facility in Wilkes-Barre, Pennsylvania. I started going to therapy again, because I knew if I didn't reach out for help sooner, later might be too late.

I was fortunate to hit it off with the therapist my doctor recommended. I started seeing her twice a week because of the bad shape I was in, mentally and emotionally. I detailed the timeline of my relationship with Roy, going over everything he's said, his unpredictable behavior, and she nodded along. I couldn't tell what she was thinking, but she didn't look surprised. I asked her if she's come across behavior like this before. She asked me if I knew what a borderline was. I've heard the term borderline personality disorder before; I knew that it was a mental illness, but I've never, to my knowledge, met someone living with it. She told me that, according to what I've told her, Roy had borderline personality disorder.

The National Institute of Mental Health defines borderline personality disorder as a mental illness marked by an ongoing pattern of varying moods, self-image, and behavior. These symptoms often result in impulsive actions and problems in relationships. My therapist explained that people with borderline have a tendency to view things in extremes, such as all good or all bad, even people, people who are friends one day, become enemies the next. They make efforts to avoid imagined abandonment by abruptly cutting of communication with someone they rapidly initiated intimacy, emotional or physical, with. I started to put it all together. She also told me that it's common with addicts, that many, if not most, are diagnosed with some form of mental illness. Conversely, some mental health conditions have also been identified as risk factors for substance use disorder.

I began to understand that Roy wasn't trying to intentionally hurt me. His version of reality—the one that I eventually started living in—cast him in the role of the victim, and assigned me with all the blame, had me apologizing for every little thing, and worse, actually believing I was at fault. I'm not saying it was his fault—mental illness is no one's fault; it's blind to its victims—however actively trying to warp other people's realities is a tell-tale sign to seek treatment. Whenever I'd suggest that he should go talk to someone like his doctor or better, a mental health professional, I was maliciously shut down. I was trying to save the wrong person this whole time.

I didn't realize how much I neglected myself to the point where I felt like an empty shell of a human. But once I started to work through my sadness and subsequent anger, I started to feel compassion towards Roy, especially as someone who also lives with mental illness.

I can't say I know exactly what he's going through, as I don't live with borderline, but I do live with, oftentimes, debilitating mental illness that I know takes a lot of work to manage. I believe that he believed I loved him, and I believe that on some level he genuinely cared about me, but I couldn't offer more than I could give without sacrificing myself in the process. I would have done anything for him— offered him a place to stay, money, rides to the appropriate resources—but ultimately, none of that would have meant anything unless he made the choice to actively want to put the work into improving his mental health and repairing his relationships. It wouldn't be long before Roy would be back in rehab again, and at that point, I could only wish him the best and remind him that I would always be there for him, as a friend, when he was ready.

After a few months of therapy, I stopped blaming myself and made the decision to stop feeling guilty about the times I shrugged it off when I would see him pop an Adderall or drink a little bit too much. It wasn't my fault. I dug myself out of the endless I-should-have-knowns I was drowning in. I tried to remember the good times we had spent together instead. He was one of the most extraordinary people I've ever met. That doesn't make what happened nor how he ended up treating me okay—far from it—but remembering his resplendent spirit, and reminding myself that he could find his way back to it, if he wants, was a way for me to start healing. But first I had to learn the hard lesson that sometimes love isn't enough, that, ultimately, he made the choice to open that door and walk through it, to spiral, and that he had to make the choice to actually want to get better, to reach out for help.

I eventually stopped talking to him because it became apparent to me that he had no interest in getting better. Even after rehab, he would slowly go back to his old ways, including contacting me out of the blue with vague threats to self-harm. He ended up moving to Denver about a year or so later. I still hear from him time to time—my therapist forecasted that he would absolutely reach back out again because people living with borderline tend to latch on to those who are or have been emotionally tethered to them—but I don't entertain any other conversation other than sending my best wishes and leaving it at that for the sake of my welfare.

It took me a few years to process everything I, we, have been through, but I'm finally in a place where I'm able to prioritize myself and my well-being, and know which relationships are worth pursuing and which are better left untouched or abandoned for the benefit of everyone involved.

I'm in a happy and healthy relationship now, and work to be the best partner I can be. My ability to love wasn't snuffed out or tarnished like I feared it would be, rather I learned how to give and receive love, unconditionally.

11. THIS YEAR'S COMIC TO WATCH (HAVE A MELTDOWN AT BOSTON MARKET)

As I continued healing from the SI unit of break-ups, nightlife slowly started to transition from a priority to an occasional night out. My focus shifted from writing for music and fashion-centered publications to writing comedy as much as I could. But before I could do that, I had to start anew.

I was still living with my parents in New Jersey, my life consisting of going to and from work, which was ten minutes north, in Princeton, at a consignment shop. I started working there the summer of my junior year at Hofstra, and I resumed working there after I graduated just to have some sort of income coming in. I was interning, remotely, for *CREEM*, but it wasn't enough. I needed a change; I was someone who liked to keep busy, to lean towards the frenetic. And what place is more frenetic than NYC?

I knew living in NYC would grant me proximity to opportunities within an industry I wanted to work in. Grad school was another idea I was toying with, since I felt like I wasn't done being a student, not just yet. And I won't say a major reason grad school appealed to me was because I could defer my undergraduate student loans, BUT I'LL TYPE IT. So, accrue more debt I did. I applied to The New School and was accepted into the Media Studies program, where I would focus on media theory and literacy. I regretted minoring in German in undergrad, which helped me become as fluent as a potato skin, so I opted minoring in something I was actually interested in learning how to do: screenwriting. Thankfully, I was privileged to receive a generous scholarship, which lessened the blow of my tuition payments, but, don't be fooled, they still stung. My job at the consignment relocated me to their recently opened location in SoHo, so the only left to do was find a place to live.

A friend of mine from Hofstra also got accepted to a graduate program at The New School, and we decided to move in together. It took us almost the entirety of summer 2014 to find an apartment because finding a place in NYC is a nightmare: there's a fee around every corner and, at the time, you had to pay first and last month's rent, a security deposit, and donate a kidney just to secure a room the size of an Ugg boot. After visiting place after place, from the bowels of Brooklyn to the crests of Manhattan, we found a home in Spanish Harlem, where we would go on to live for two years until the Q line was extended to four blocks away from our apartment and our rent went up by $35 million dollars.

The semester started and I continued my internship with CREEM. I was, for the most part, assigned to interview artists: painters, illustrators, graphic designers, mixed media mavens, you name it. Here's the thing: I'm not from the art world. Truth be told, I don't know how to tell if art is good or bad. What is a brush stroke, a gradient? My knowledge of painting starts and stops at Microsoft Paint. I used to paint flowers and birds as a kid, BUT I WAS, LIKE, EIGHT. There's a reason why my brother's illustrations and paintings

are hung all over the house—HINT: HE'S A PROFES-
SIONAL ARTIST—and all my paintings of robins and
chickadees are relegated to the shitter. "It's just a coinci-
dence," said my mom. And then, conveniently, the next time
I came home, one of my "paintings" was moved to the guest
room. Behind a book shelf.

I wanted to riff with my subjects. Just because they were
artists doesn't mean they had to take themselves seriously all
the time. I wanted to be like Joan Rivers, asking funny questions to actors on the red carpet at the Academy Awards. One
time I interviewed a quasi-famous artist known for her brazen
and humorous paintings and mixed media art. When my
editor assigned the piece, I thought we'd be a match made in
heaven. I was supposed to interview her about her recent
exhibit, which featured Chanel bags made from things like
pancakes and baguettes, with the iconic (and the only non-
edible element) Chanel logo affixed. I loved it. I couldn't wait
to talk to her because I knew you had to have a pretty special
sense of humor to put something out like that into a world
that's not necessarily known for taking itself not so seriously.

I started the interview with an innocuous joke, I think it
was something along the lines of, "which Applebee's two-for-
twenty menu combo do you think would yield the sturdiest
material for a handbag?"

I was met with a blank stare.

After a beat, she just went, "no."

Before I could be like, "I'M OUT," my editor started
assigning me musicians. I interviewed Marina and the
Diamonds, Estelle, and my first cover story was an interview
with rapper Brooke Candy. I clicked with each of them,
finally finding a way to marry my editorial voice with my
comedic propensity. Other editors started to take notice.
Within a year, I was commissioned to write three cover

stories. I had my words published in print from Los Angeles to Denver to an erotic literary journal in London (don't be fooled, my essay for that was about as sexy as a deflated air mattress, but I was still proud to be published in print, nonetheless!).

My friend, Justin, asked me if I wanted to start writing for *BULLETT*, a now-defunct online magazine that he was the digital managing editor of at the time. I was a fan of *BULLETT* and wrote my first humor piece for them that lead to many others. With Justin's encouragement, I was able to lean into my craft and experiment with different forms and styles, nurturing my voice and learning how to adapt it to a specific type of publication and audience.

Eventually, *Out* Magazine gave me my own satirical column, which I wrote for a year.

Okay, cool, yeah, looks great on paper, right? But here's the thing: I view anyone else's success as a personal attack. If you're twenty-two, you are, by default, my enemy, and I must vanquish you. Any high I derived from seeing my by-line would immediately be extinguished by finding out *GQ* did a write-up on a twenty-one-year-old comedian, proclaiming them as that year's comic-to-watch when I was well into my mid-twenties and still on a family plan. This is, of course, is not a healthy way of thinking and the fastest way to living a life devoid of joy, ESPECIALLY WHEN YOU ARE ONLY TWENTY-SIX.

I was the enemy here, not anyone else who was probably working just as hard (if not harder!) to achieve the write-ups, TV writing gigs, and various other accolades they deserve. I couldn't acknowledge the fast track I was on. Any objective human could tell I was well on my way to becoming the writer I strived to be. I just didn't see it.

My self-doubt grew up alongside me, a little voice whispering, "you're not good enough," into my teenage ear, to yelling, "NO ONE CARES WHAT YOU HAVE TO SAY," into my ear now. I thought my potential stopped at the ability to be seen and liked, that I was this glittering personality who wore unique clothes and occasionally made people laugh with anecdotes on Facebook or on my silly little blog. I thought that by asking people to actually listen and absorb what I had to say—to have a voice—was asking for *too* much. In many ways, I still felt like the young kid who always struggled to be heard, who was never loud or assertive enough.

Well, I was loud now, at least visually I knew I could grab someone's attention just by virtue of my physical appearance; I just needed to figure out how to hold it. Like spraying stencils in my hair and going to a party in the Lower East Side, I knew I had to make an impression in this new world I wanted to become a part of. AND BOY DID I.

That winter one of my best friends, Nikki, invited me to a networking event for people in publishing. At the time, she worked at a publisher of textbooks, so she was in the loop about any industry-related events. It was basically a wine and cheese night held at an event space on the third floor at Penguin Random House. After mingling with marketing assistants and the person tasked with bringing out more cheese, I noticed an author whose book I really enjoyed in the crowd. I was feeling confident because I already made some connections and felt like maybe, just maybe, I could belong among these people, even if I was wearing red, patent leather pointed-toe boots with a leopard-print bandana tied around one leg.

I approached the author and introduced myself, complimenting her on her recent release and telling her I'm a fan of her writing. She thanked me and asked me what I was doing there, at the networking event.

"Uh, isn't it obvious, there's cheese," I joked.

She laughed, and, feeling the initial awkwardness dissipate, I told her I wanted to write a book one day. There was an awkward pause before she was like, "Oh! Wow, I never would have thought that about you!"

I wanted to immediately stop, drop and roll out of there. I was there to make a few contacts, sure, but more importantly, absorb all that I could from being in that environment and learn a few things along the way, but I left that night feeling like I was rejected by a boy I had a crush on. I was met with many looks that essentially translated to "why is it here????," so I would just helicopter over the cheese plate and watch from afar. I could have just worn my hair down and slicked it to the side and threw on a modest sweater with a pair of khakis to match, but I liked my hair and clothes. I didn't want to sacrifice one part of who I was for a part of who I was to become; I believed they could co-exist.

The next publishing-related event I went to was a social mixer for the humor writers of a Very Reputable Publication. If you're a humor writer, or basically a writer of any kind, this magazine is one of the most coveted publications to get your work published in, and it can be hard to do so without an agent or knowing someone who knows someone.

My friend, Abby, whose submission was recently accepted and published in said publication, was invited to the mixer and asked me if I wanted to go with her. I was elated. This was my chance to connect with the best-of-the-best in the business.

I was tempted to just fill the inside of a trench coat with a dozen samples of writing so when I met an editor, I could open my coat to display the various pieces I've written and ask them if they were interested in one like I'm selling a bunch of pirated Blu-ray DVDs of *Gigli*. Instead, I printed several copies of my work in addition to a bunch of my business cards.

First mistake.

Business cards are fine, many people carry them, but WHO SHOWS UP TO A FANCY EVENT WITH A BUNCH OF XEROXED COPIES OF A HUMOR PIECE CALLED "THE GAY COUSIN'S HOLIDAY SURVIVAL GUIDE" AND PASS THEM OUT LIKE A BUNCH OF FLYERS TO A COMEDY SHOW?

Where is the nearest lake so I can walk directly into it????

We got to the bar and it was probably the most accurate representation of a bar in Brooklyn I've ever seen. It was set up taverna-style, adorned from wall to wall in rustic bric-a-brac and other whimsical items one would buy in a hut by the sea, candles in jars that looked like they were props from a Hogwarts classroom, and an ambience that could only be found inside a lava lamp. The crowd only substantiated the heavy Brooklyn vibe: everyone was decked out in earth tones and had on black, thick-framed prescription glasses. I don't even think I was at a mixer as much as the set of *Girls*.

With no one wanting a copy of my "comedy zine," I planted myself at the bar.

I stood out in the sea of sensible, argyle-monopolized sweaters with collars popping out at the top with my larger-than-life polka dots and sparkly shoes that, if I tapped together and repeated, "there's no place like home," would transport me back in time to Studio 54. I met a few people who were willing to engage in some small talk, but for the most part I felt like an interloper. It's not unlike how I've felt at certain parties in the nightlife circuit. Here I am, trying to present myself as a young professional while trying to be myself and the only question I got asked that night was, "did your shoes come like that?" I felt like Elle Woods at Harvard for the first time, wanting to belong in a place where you wouldn't expect to find someone like me.

Maybe I was taking too big of a leap, I thought after that night. I had cast my net too wide, and I had to reel it back in. I had to take baby steps. Back to the nightlife scene I went, but not the one I've found a home in, but a new sector: the comedy circuit.

12. FROM CLUB KID TO COMEDY WRITER

At first, I started by just attending shows—stand-up, improv, reading series—and observing how everything went down. I spent my evenings watching comedians and actors perform from the Upright Citizens Brigade to the Comedy Cellar, and wondered what my role in this world could be. From those shows, I collected flyers and perused Facebook for future shows to attend.

My first comedian friend, Claudia Cogan, invited me to a comedy show she was performing at that's every second Wednesday of the month at Beauty Bar on Fourteenth Street. I love Beauty Bar for two reasons: 1. My friends and I frequently end our nights there with a nightcap, and 2. It's right next door to the only IHOP in Manhattan, and I have no problem extolling the superior quality of IHOP's chicken fingers but my editors want me to keep the chicken finger references down to a dull roar.

I attended the upcoming comedy show at Beauty Bar on the following month's second Wednesday solo, which was hosted by Negin Farsad, author of one of my favorite books called *How to Make White People Laugh*. I watched my friend Claudia do her set, and she, of course, killed. Claudia, who is also friends with Negin, introduced me, and Negin couldn't have been nicer. She was generous with her time, detailing every step of the book publishing process, which, if I'm being honest, MADE ME WANT TO DIE.

Not only would I have to write a book, but also there was a proposal, a platform, marketing, and a thousand other things to take into consideration and then my head exploded. Negin was completely awe-inspiring and I left that comedy night feeling half motivated and half I'LL NEVER BE ABLE TO DO THIS. I shared a bill with her a few years later at Claudia's comedy show in Brooklyn, where Claudia asked me to read one of my satirical columns from *Out*. I didn't tell anyone at the time, but it was my first time reading something I wrote to an audience. I had to work on slowing down and pausing for laughs. But I got laughs, and that's all I cared about.

The rest was just practice.

This was a step I could take. But now, I had one foot in nightlife, and another in comedy. And it's not like the two often crossed paths. Sure, there are drag shows, which are campy by nature, but there weren't many nightlife personalities I could commiserate over putting together a book proposal with. And there weren't many comedians I came across who would accompany me to M&J Trimming to pick out studs to bedazzle a bandana with.

It was like being pulled in two different directions. I felt too docile for one and too eccentric for the other. Nightlife was special to me. It still is, even if nowadays when I say I'm going out, I mean to the nearest bookstore. But the more serious I became about pursuing comedy writing, the less tethered to nightlife I became.

Eventually, I started to feel like an outsider among club kids because my change in direction was pointing me towards an industry that seldom intersects with the world of bottle service and intensely hued eyeshadow. It was time to make my exit. Comedy satisfied something deeper than nightlife. Comedy was, and still is, what sates me more than anything else. It has, quite literally, saved my life.

I was going through an-almost-quarter-life-crisis and a severe bout of depression. I stumbled upon Megan Amram's Tumblr, on a satirical piece called, "Paula Deen's Health Food Cookbook," and stayed up all night until I read and re-read every one of her pieces, tears in my eyes from laughter, which was a nice change from TEARS OF NEVERENDING WORRY AND DESPAIR. I let myself fall to sleep that night with the respite of knowing that Megan's blog would still be there in the morning, and the next day, and that I could always return to the laughter when everything else seemed like a giant abysmal mass of terrible.

I stopped praying for the earth to open up and swallow me whole every morning and continued writing humor pieces, and THANK GOD, because there isn't anything else I could do or offer this world. (My mom had expressed, at one point, that she wanted me to become a pharmacist. If her dream came true your Zoloft refill would definitely contain, like, two rogue Skittles.) I started to meet other stand-up comedians, comedy writers, and authors, most of whom were incredibly sweet and generous with their advice—to keep submitting, to not be discouraged by rejection, to not give up —and even offering to read my work and provide me with feedback.

I met Sloane Crosley at a book signing at the Barnes and Noble in Union Square and basically squealed in her face for thirty seconds straight. A few years later, I would go on to meet and befriend my, truly, favorite writer of all time, the treasure Samantha Irby, after going to her book launch in Brooklyn last April. The fact that we text almost every day still hasn't registered to me, even though we've been friends for over a year now.

It was these types of interactions I was hungry for, to live in a city where they become a part of your day-to-day life. You could meet someone you've admired sitting at a bar next to you: there was a night I met Debbie fucking Harry at a party for Molly Ringwald. It was surreal, magical, and always a reminder of why I fell in love with New York in the first place.

I was getting positive feedback from friends and followers on Twitter on my satiric pieces and articles that made fun of events in pop culture (that's not to say there was some heinous shit in the comments, but that's a writer's rite-of-passage no matter what you're writing about. You can write about the benefits of knitting and @toby1938327382 will be like, DIE IN A FIRE). A few of my columns went viral, one of which, entitled "First Look: Olsen Twins Release a Line of Wiccan Supplies and Accessories," accumulated over 40,000 shares in just one day.

It felt like a sign that I was heading in the right direction, that there was room in the market for me and my brand of humor and style of writing and if not, I would always find my own way in. If not through the front door, then I would slip in through the side or crawl in through an air duct like Bruce Willis in *Die Hard*.

I was able to mitigate the self-doubt I've been plagued with up until that point. It's not totally absent from my life: I

still find myself comparing myself to other writers, comedians, even going through days where I haven't written
anything and wonder if I'll ever be able to produce something
funny ever again. But the best way to silence that voice in my
head is by doing the work and listening for the laughs.

13. 25 TWEETS THAT UNDERPERFORMED SO I'M IMMORTALIZING THEM IN THIS BOOK OUT OF SPITE

1. "If It Makes You Happy" by Sheryl Crow is about eating two dinners, right?

2. Went to Medieval Times and didn't get dysentery—I WANT A REFUND.

3. Should I go to my ten-year high school reunion, or should I just wear a short-sleeve shirt over a long-sleeve shirt that day?

4. I don't mean to brag, but after taking a bath, drinking two cups of chamomile tea, and applying a generous helping of lavender essential oils, I'm still anxious.

5. How do you report relatives who give you birthday cards without money for spam?

6. Is it true that if I put a Yankee Candle at each point of a pentagram I'll summon Enya?

7. FYI, I'm always looking for a friend-with-benefits.* ;)

*Someone who owns a printer.

8. My business card is just the Tarot card that represents Death.

9. I want my gravestone to read: "connect to power source."

10. Is there a support group for people who've abused the mantra "treat yoself"?

11. My emotional support alpaca bit someone at Au Bon Pain again.

12. My coven put me on probation because I substituted a sage stick with a mozzarella stick.

13. Phrases I've heard an elevator technician say that my therapist has also used to describe my mental health:
-"Unstable"
-"Performing at a limited capacity"
-"Damaged beyond repair"

14. My last boyfriend broke up with me because instead of moaning his name during sex, I moaned my Grubhub discount code.

15. Oh, you love me? Name 500 people I can't stand.

16. I wonder who's gonna catch my bouquet of Outback Steakhouse Bloomin' Onion at my wedding.

17. What's this scar from, you ask? I pronounced the "x" in "LaCroix" at Whole Foods and someone threw a pineapple at me.

18. I panicked and told my mom my sex bruises were the result of a freak accident involving a runaway hot dog cart.

19. Guess I'm officially the-only-person-who-texts-me-on-a-Friday-night-is-CVS-telling-me-my-prescription-is-ready years old.

20. Auditioned for *Law & Order* by just steering saying, "call me when you have something," and now I've been cast as next season's new ADA.

21. Me: I'M TIRED ALL THE TIME
Doctor: Are you getting enough sleep?
Me: No
Doctor: Do you eat right?
Me: No
Doctor: Do you exercise?
Me: JUST TELL ME THAT I HAVE AN IRON DEFICIENCY.

22. Upstaging the other gay cousin at Christmas by wearing Ferrero Rocher wrappers as nipple pasties.

23. I JUST got drinks with someone fourteen months ago, and they already want to go out for drinks AGAIN.

24. Had a sex dream about owning a rolling library ladder.

25. Getting a book deal is 5% celebrating and 95% wondering how you're going to break it to your parents that you write about how some dude's jizz tasted like flat Diet Sprite.

14. THE THANKLESS TRIFECTA: EVERY JOB A CREATIVE SHOULD HAVE

I'm a published author now, with a real book out in the world and everything, and my primary source of income comes from my job as an administrative assistant for a Lutheran church in downtown Brooklyn. I just switched my health insurance for the THIRD FUCKING TIME in one year. I can't afford to write full-time because, as of today, I am owed over $3,300 in freelance fees. Granted, a large majority of that money is due from one outlet, which has recently been in the news for not paying forty-eight of its contributors—your boy included—over the last year. To say it's been a shit-show would be a profound understatement.

The reality is I'll probably never see that money because it's going to draw out in court for the rest of eternity or until whenever this planet implodes because the Right cares more about buoying corporate power structures that comes at the cost of our rapidly declining environment than, I don't know, BREATHING. The remaining $300? That's just recent fees I won't see until I follow-up no fewer than eighty-two times over the span of ten months. You would be surprised how difficult it is for a major media conglomerate to pay a free-lancer a measly $250—peanuts for them!—but I have an email thread longer than a CVS receipt to prove just how much of a production it is.

I'm in my late twenties, and I'm just now getting the hang of juggling my writing, day job(s), and any other odd jobs I can snag for some extra cash. I still won't be using "summer" as a verb anytime soon, but at least I trust myself to land on my feet anytime the rug of employment is pulled out from beneath me, which has been often. But before finding this balance—or as close to balanced as I can be—I struggled through long hours, tears, disappointment, panic, anxiety, depression, overwhelming fatigue, ups, downs, and every-thing in between in order to even start on the path I wanted to see myself on. This is all on top of *finding* the time to work on the things I hoped will blossom into the reality I wished to create for myself. And I'm white, cisgender, able-bodied, and was, even though I grew up lower middle class, still afforded the opportunity to go to a good public high school by virtue of my zip code. If I were Black or brown, I would have to work twice as hard to only get half as far because of the systemic barriers that exasperate the vicious cycle of wealth inequality and thwart people of color from achieving the same socioeco-nomic advantages as their white counterparts. That's reality. This country's and mine, because, like the system, I TOO AM BROKE.

Like my friend and writer Sara Benincasa says: real artists have day jobs.

I've found through my own experience that there are three type of jobs every person pursuing a career in a creative industry—in my case, being a writer—that is seldom lucrative from the start. They're gigs I believe teach you valuable lessons that will inevitably become handy in whatever you pursue.

I like to call them "The Thankless Trifecta": restaurant, retail, and office. I've done them all. I've also been TERRIBLE at each one, and I mean *TERRIBLE*. Despite my lack of skills in each of these fields, I'm glad I worked at each place because each one gave me a reality check I needed. And by reality check, I mean confirmed that I definitely better make this writing thing work because my skill set is limited.

RESTAURANT

I didn't have this job in NYC, but I did start working at the age of sixteen at a restaurant in Princeton, New Jersey, about ten minutes away from my parents' house. It was my first job. I was excited to finally have my own source of income because it made me feel important, even though I was only getting paid $5.50 an hour, plus twenty percent of tips split evenly between the other bussers. I could finally say, "sorry, I can't, I have to work" while my unemployed friends went out for water ice. Oh, young naïve sixteen-year-old Greg, little did you know you would be saying that phrase lot in the future sans the enthusiastic attitude behind it and wishing your mouth could be stained red from a strawberry water ice.

I was what they called an "assistant server," which was just a glorified busboy. On my first night, a Saturday night, I dropped an entire tray of empty wine glasses in the middle of the restaurant. All the servers reassured me that it happens to everyone, that this rookie mistake is a rite-of-passage for anyone working in the service industry, but it happened to me at least once a week for the three years I worked there.

I kept that job for two summers when I came home for break from college. One summer I went to a Lady Gaga concert and, like any sane person who attends one of her concerts, I wore some sort of ensemble that included ripped tights, a crop-top, and fashioned some caution tape into a headband. This was hot on the heels of the "Telephone" video, so caution tape was en vogue. Ostensibly my friends and I took 10,000 pictures because what else was going to make me cringe in ten years when Facebook reminds me what happened on that day?

I was tagged in a handful of them on Facebook and when I came into work a few days later, I heard the other busboys whispering and suddenly become quiet once I came within earshot. They would take turns coming up to me and creepily whisper, "ra ra, rah ah ah," in my ear. I put two and two together and realized one of the servers I befriended added me on Facebook and probably showed the busboys all the photos of me because they all lived in the same house just a few blocks away. Anytime I walked past them I would hear them burst into laughter. I didn't need to speak Spanish to know what they were saying about me; getting called a faggot has the same sting in any language. They would ask me where my tights and panties were every time I clocked in for my shift, and I would just awkwardly laugh along while I fantasized about quitting and walking out while the restaurant explodes in flames behind me like Angela Bassett walking away from that exploding car in *Waiting to Exhale*.

I made a few friends working there but for the most part the staff consisted of a bunch of student teachers from The College of New Jersey who talked shit about the other servers and fought over who would serve the Princeton professor who came in every Saturday and always left a twenty-dollar tip even though he only ordered a salad and a water. There was always petty drama and I would spend the majority of my shifts avoiding getting caught in the crossfire.

The clientele wasn't much better: it was mostly a bunch of uptight businessmen and their wives who I'm convinced were just a bunch of sentient shawls from Ann Taylor who would throw fits because the ramekin their salad dressing was served in didn't match their desired salad-to-dressing ratio. I wouldn't know what to do when someone yelled at me because their Moroccan salmon wasn't the exact temperature they requested or they wanted seven ice cubes in their sangria and NOT eight. I would apologize under my breath and promise to let their server know, but instead I went out back and dry-heaved into the phone to my mom. I dropped plates left and right and ate the fries in the kitchen whenever the head chef would turn the other way. I developed a smoking habit.

RETAIL

Ah, the most character-building out of them all. Working retail is a feat—no matter what you're selling. I was already working retail at a high-end consignment boutique before I moved to NYC so when I moved, I transferred to their SoHo location and quickly became the assistant manager. The best thing about this job was the wealth of friends I gained from it; many of my co-workers from this job have become friends of the lifelong variety. As for the job itself, well, I did about as well as I did working in a restaurant.

First of all, if you've worked retail, you know the smile you have to feign when you just broke up with someone and the pleasantness you have to force when some impatient schmuck is yelling at you because they want to return something even though you have a noticeable sign not unlike a Broadway marquee next to the register that says **ALL SALES ARE FINAL.**

It was grueling and my patience was running out quick. I started to clock in late (not that I had a stellar record of clocking in on time to begin with, I was probably busy teaching myself Fosse choreography!) and did the minimal effort needed not to get fired. I needed the money even though the pay was only a dollar more than my hourly wage in the other location, the one in New Jersey, which in New York is basically worth as much as Kohl's Cash, but I was terrified of "getting comfortable" at this job. I had nightmares that I would be tagging clothing and negotiating a ten percent discount on a pair of Ferragamo shoes the customer claims is smudged despite there being no smudge to the naked eye.

I knew this job was only temporary because you have to take any job in order to keep your head above water in a city like New York. Working there became insufferable because we were losing employees left and right—they either quit or were fired—and running the store came down to just three of us. I started working an average of almost forty hours a week —full-time!—in addition to being a student and a writer. I would have multiple meltdowns in the back room because it was becoming too much, too quickly. I had to work doubles because we didn't have enough staff to schedule one person to open the store, and another to close it. Due to a lack of employees, I was opening AND closing a store that was open from ten to nine almost four days a week, sometimes more.

I felt my grip on school and writing slip because all of the time and energy I was investing into a job with a corporate office that ignored our requests for things like basic transparency and being treated with respect. The owner of the company and her minions (whom I secretly referred to as "The Tribunal") had a blatant disregard for their SoHo employees, two of whom were twenty-somethings (myself included) balancing school and other responsibilities, and another a mother of two. I would argue her children required more attention than some woman named Barbara pitching a bitch fit because we didn't have an item in stock, despite us repeating over and over that we're a consignment shop, MEANING THERE'S ONLY ONE OF EVERYTHING.

Raises would not be considered outside of the yearly evaluation, and if we did qualify for a raise, it wouldn't be more than a dollar. The starting wage as a retail associate, in the SoHo location, was only eleven dollars an hour. This was before New York State made the minimum wage fifteen dollars an hour, and even that's a struggle to get by on for most people, especially in a state where you have to put up a lung in collateral if you can't afford your wildly exorbitant rent.

The three of us ran the store by ourselves for about five months until we found that corporate was closing the SoHo location because we weren't making enough money to cover our rent. They failed to take into account that the shoppers in our neighborhood could easily afford brand-new, off-the-runway Chanel from the Chanel boutique that was located just around the corner. No one was interested in purchasing second-hand Ann Taylor and Eileen Fischer from two years ago when they could buy it brand new just a hop and a skip away. We constantly made suggestions, encouraging a rebrand, a fresher way of doing things in the New York location that would have to shy away from how the other locations were doing things, reminding them that their SoHo shoppers were different from their other shoppers in New Jersey and Pennsylvania, but they fell on deaf ears. The news of our store closing was like a punch in stomach. We were given virtually no notice. They made the decision to close the store in January. They waited until May to tell us...that the store would close at the end of that month, on the 31st! I suspected they waited to the very last minute to tell us so we wouldn't go off and find another job and abandon an already sinking ship.

We got laid off, which actually ended up being a blessing in disguise because we were all so burnt out we couldn't handle it anymore. I collected my less-than-impressive severance check and vowed never to work retail again if I could help it. There was only one problem: I was unemployed.

OFFICE ASSISTANT

After I was laid off from the consignment shop, I had a lot of free time on my hands because the semester ended and I was still, obviously, unemployed. I decided to start a really big writing project—hint: it's the one you're reading right now. I still needed a job because, unfortunately, I'm not the heir to the Burt's Bees empire.

I sought a campus job at The New School. I thought working at school might make things a little easier. Class and work were super close to each other, and I could use the time I would have spent commuting to a different job writing. I was hired as an administrative assistant, even though I showed up to the interview visibly hungover (I forgot to take my sunglasses off until five minutes into the interview), with a club stamp on my hand. I white-knuckled my interview, and SOME THE FUCK HOW, got hired????

My responsibilities included the typical administrative tasks as an office assistant: answering phone calls, managing people's schedules, greeting people when they come into the reception area, among other administrative tasks. I performed these tasks with the same enthusiasm my older brother exhibited when my parents made him include me in his playtime activities as a little kid.

In between these duties, I was warming up a Lean Cuisine in the communal kitchen as I silently prayed for 6pm/death—whichever came first. Also, when I said I was attentive to detail in my interview and efficient, I actually meant the opposite. I'm pretty sure I still have a remote student from Florida on hold to speak to an academic advisor. Oh, I have to complete this spreadsheet by noon? On it! Right after I take an hour-long break at The Strand. Also, sorry I got SmartFood white cheddar popcorn dust on your xeroxed syllabi.

I was perpetually frustrated because I wasn't making money doing what I wanted to be doing. I was getting paid twelve dollars an hour to be reminded by the assistant events coordinator that she was vegan. I had a co-worker who called me ten seconds after sending me an email to let me know she had sent me an email. Office politics and drama bubbled to the surface daily. Thankfully, I wasn't working at this position full-time, so I could juggle the various other writing projects I had put on my plate. If things were slow in the office, I could get my homework done and get a head start on whatever writing I was working on: an essay, script, this book, which I wrote about seventy percent of during my time at this job.

The good thing about working as an office assistant as a student was that I could write all day long at my desk when I wasn't answering calls, which sort of felt like I was a professional writer with an office and a desk, except my paycheck could barely cover a fountain soda at the movies.

I managed to make it work. I made it my priority to strike a balance because I still wanted to have time to pursue my creative ambitions, no matter how much this job, the passive aggressive emails from co-workers, and the angry students (and sometimes parents) drained me. After two years at that job, I was forced to leave it after I graduated because the position could only be held by matriculating students.

Unemployed as I was, again, I was still working—for free. I took on almost every writing opportunity that came my way, which only resulted in a loss of time, and, ergo, money. Some gigs paid, but it wasn't enough to forfeit a biweekly paycheck for full-time freelancing. I was overpaying my dues at this point, when I should have spent my time looking for something stable. It was like perpetually walking up the down escalator: I was stuck, constantly trying to climb my way up, and failing.

If I was ever going to gain momentum making money doing the thing I love, I had to learn how to say no.

15. NO MORE MR. "YEAH, I GUESS I CAN DO THAT FOR FREE THIS TIME" GUY

Kathy Griffin once made a joke on her Bravo reality show, *My Life on the D-List,* about how a typical week in her life as a D-list celebrity is selling out Carnegie Hall one week, and, in that same week, book a commercial for a chain of fried chicken joints somewhere in the south. A typical week in my life as a freelance writer would be getting my pitch accepted at *Vanity Fair* one day, and the next, interview an up-and-coming band from Tennessee called something like The Sexual Pen Pals for the inaugural issue of an LA-based zine that pays in Hulu passwords.

People told me that I can pursue what I love to do "on the side," but that school and work came first, like my dreams were the optional salad bar at Ruby Tuesday. Yes, I put school high on my list of priorities, of course I did, especially since I was lucky enough to qualify for a generous scholarship, but I didn't sacrifice comfort for calamity to be the assistant manager at a retail store whose corporate office treated their employees like the pretzels on a shelf of discounted Halloween candy. So I said yes, to everything. I couldn't say no; I didn't know how.

My insatiable appetite for exposure cost me—literally. I basically had to perform a self-exorcism to rid the demon that is naivety from my body. Also, I was ashamed. I was embarrassed, especially when someone like a friend or a close family member would respond to my news of getting my writing published with, "that's great—how much are they paying you?"

I took this as an act of aggression instead of the registering that someone, like my brother, who has first-hand experience lending his expertise in illustration and graphic design to a bounty of friends who promised they would compensate him once whatever they were working on took off, yet seldom saw anything resembling payment, even when a decent-sized budget was achieved, was asking this question from a place of concern and cautious optimism. As someone prone to leading with emotion, I lashed out. I disguised my embarrassment under the guise of anger. I was like, "UH, I JUST INTERVIEWED [minor celebrity] AND HAVE A BY-LINE IN [glossy magazine that's on newsstands that definitely cost a lot of money to produce, yet said magazine claims that there's "no budget" to pay a freelance writer] AND INSTEAD OF BEING IMPRESSED, YOU ONLY CARE ABOUT WHAT I'M [definitely not] MAKING?

It was the same naivety that told me to take on every assignment, paid or not. I would meekly ask if there was a budget—the answer was, more times than not, no—and I would still write the essay or do the interview, because I firmly believe that that one assignment would be the one to open all the doors for me, and behind one of those doors would be a bigger, better publican with a budget, one with benefits and monetary compensation instead of the promise of a free drink or a regifted gift card to Walgreens.

This led to getting taken advantage of, even by friends. I was naïve enough to think that my friendship with someone would act as insurance of me getting paid down the line. I had an editor, who was a friend first, who promised me for two years that they'd do everything in their power to get me on the payroll. I would submit invoice after invoice, and then payment was promised week, after month, after yearly quarter, after year, until, eventually, I just gave up asking if I would be paid for TWO YEARS' WORTH OF WORK. In the end, I ended up over-drafting, on money and self-respect.

I also gave my internship the benefit of the doubt when my gut told me to do the opposite. I had a vision that in six months I could fulfill my ultimate dream: getting paid to work from home. Unfortunately, reality seldom mirrors the fantasy. If the walls could talk, they'd ask, "HOW MANY EPISODES OF *TOP CHEF* CAN YOU WATCH IN A ROW?" The reality was that I was working for free, in T-shirt I haven't bothered to change in seventy-two hours, sending my resumé and cover letter out through hundreds of online portals only to yield a ratio of fifty applications to one interview. I was home, but I wasn't getting paid for my time and labor.

I met up with my friend, Mika, at a bar to drown my freelance sorrows in bottom-shelf whiskey and get some advice. Mika's been an active participant in the gig economy for over a decade. After a few drinks, he laid down some hard truths I needed to hear: if I continue to work for free, continue saying yes to unpaid work, the easier it is for people to take advantage of me and my talent, and worse, continue their reign of unpaid terror on more people. I wasn't just fucking myself, but I was also preventing others who do charge for their work up front (another rule I learned: require a deposit before taking on a job) from a paid opportunity. I was possibly hurting other writers, photographers, graphic designers, and anyone else in demand in the world of freelance. By putting a foot down and saying no to unpaid work, I'm doing a favor for myself and my colleagues. It also helps our community of creatives maintain a network: we know whom to steer clear from and who actually values (and budgets for) the free-lancers they hire.

My time is valuable. And if I want to waste it on things like mindless television or designing a line of Celtic cloaks for my cat, that's up to me. But unless we're related or boning, I won't work for free, bye!

16. MOMENTS THAT REMINDED ME I LIVE IN NYC

Sometimes it's easy to forget that you live in one of the most magical, residentially coveted cities in the world. Your chaotic schedule can blind you to the ordinary, everyday beauty in your periphery, but every so often you're reminded that you live in a city that serves as a backdrop for every third movie and TV show. Below are some of my favorite, "Wow, I live in NYC" moments that I would like to share with you to remind you why it's so easy to fall in love with this majestic city:

- I saw a woman stop the subway doors from closing by using a baby carriage. The baby was in it.

- One time a homeless man struck up a conversation with my backpack.

- I witnessed someone giving someone a hand job on horse carriage ride in Central Park.

- No, it wasn't me.

- I threw a tantrum that registered at 6.3 on the Richter scale when I found out I was four blocks out of delivery range for freshly baked cookies.

- I saw a tourist stop the subway doors from closing by using a selfie stick.

- I called the freshly baked cookie delivery service and offered a generous tip for making the extra four-block pilgrimage.

- They said no and I threatened to write a scathing Yelp review.

- Accepting defeat, they begrudgingly delivered freshly baked cookies to my doorstep.

- I successfully negotiated delivery terms for freshly baked cookies.

- One week I was so busy I had to block out a time slot for a meltdown on my Google calendar.

- On my packed subway commute home one night, an old woman literally yelled at me for being tall.

- Two best friends WHO SHALL REMAIN UNNAMED went door to door in one of the friend's apartment building asking each tenant if they had any Xanax like they were neighbors asking to borrow a cup of sugar.

- I went into an artisanal coffee shop in the West Village that had six different types of recycling receptacles.

- I saw a man put his cigarette out in a Salvation Army donation bucket during the holidays.

- A homeless man tried to sell me a leaf in Union Square.

- I once saw a shaman walking around Penn Station burning sage.

- I walked by a cluster of police officers standing outside a restaurant investigating a stabbing during brunch.

- I lived a year in an apartment without knowing what my neighbor looked like.

- I was having coffee in Central Park with a friend at ten a.m. and witnessed an older man, wearing a tattered hat and 3D glasses (the red and blue ones) in lieu of sunglasses, pushing a wheelchair filled with a huge bag of recycling and talking to said huge bag.

- A homeless woman rejected the food I offered to give her because she said she's gluten-free.

17. LIBIDNOPE: A STORY OF UNINTENTIONAL CHASTITY

After my relationship with Roy, I ended up not having sex for three and a half years.

Three and a half years! THAT'S 38.9 YEARS IN GAY YEARS.

My therapist was helping me navigate the major changes I made in my life after my relationship with Roy imploded, like moving to NYC and starting grad school. With time, I established a new routine—school, work, writing—and struck a balance between the three. I started to focus my emotional work on finding out why my ability to be intimate, to give myself to another person, both physically and mentally, had been impaired.

I realized my issues with intimacy weren't even rooted in sex, rather from something much more visceral. I let Roy see what I *really* looked like: I wasn't this larger-than-life character with him, the night-lifer whom I loved to inhabit. When I was with Roy, I let go of that artifice. Artifice can be a beautiful tool, empowering and liberating. But I let myself be vulnerable with him: I let my hair down, literally and metaphorically, allowed him to see me without the clothes I used as armor, the hair I styled sky-high. I pranced around his room and Pratt's campus in his hoodies and my hair in a top knot. I loved that I could show him all of me. It was this sense of totality I was after, and I finally achieved it with him. The walls I had put up as a result of the subsequent damage done to our trust did more harm than good.

I had to learn that being vulnerable wasn't a bad thing, rather it took strength, something which I thought putting a guard up would give me, when, in fact, it did the opposite. I slowly started to heal, and with that, became more open to meeting new people, romantic or otherwise.

And then it came—NOT ME—but a howling crevasse of sexual frustration. I needed to get laid. I wanted to be spontaneous, but that was something I've never indulged in, not even in college, which, in between a college campus and the nightlife scene, presented me with an endless buffet of dick. Because this is my memoir and I can be petty if I want to: I blame David.

The first time I saw David was at the beginning of my fall semester in 2011, coming out of the twenty-four-hour campus deli. We made immediate eye contact and couldn't stop staring at each other. Imagine that moment of kismet a few nights later when my friend, Markeya, texted me to ask if she could invite a friend over that night to watch *Jersey Shore* with us in my room and that friend ended up being David. When they showed up at my door I almost dropped the glass of wine I had in my hand. We both immediately blushed when she introduced us.

After a few more friends came over to watch that night's

episode of *Jersey Shore* (shut up, you watched it, too), David and I sat next to each other on my bed, sneaking glances at each other. While Snooki talked about her affinity for pickles while sitting in a mini fridge, the tension between us became palpable. By the end of the episode, his hand was on my knee, and my arms were around his shoulders. Everyone immediately came up with excuses to leave before MTV could even air a preview of next week's episode, leaving us alone.

We ended up making out, first in my room, then outside on a bench, until four in the morning.

David turned out to be my first love, and the first time I was having sex consistently with someone I trusted and loved. By the time December rolled around, I told him that I was ready to take the next step, that I wanted to make it official and be in a relationship with him. I thought he felt the same way, since literally everyone we knew always referred to the other as Greg or David's boyfriend. He felt...the opposite.

I was heartbroken; he was my first love, so of course it tore me to pieces. I completely fell apart over the holiday break when he texted me to say he was sorry, that he had met someone. He had a boyfriend now. I was more pissed than upset, especially since, just a few weeks ago, he explicitly told me he was "not the relationship type."

A few weeks after he told me he had a boyfriend, we met up at Down the Hatch, a bar in the Village that my friend Tommy was working at that night. He told me he'd broken up with his boyfriend after he found out that he had cheated on him. I cried, told him how much he'd hurt me and he apologized, and we eventually reconciled. We spent the night making out and drinking. For a night, I thought we could start where we left off.

He erased himself from my life, again, when he didn't

return to Hofstra for the spring semester because of issues pertaining to his financial aid. He told me our reunion the other night at Down the Hatch was a mistake, that he still wanted his space. I found myself heartbroken, again, but now, looking back, we were both so young—not even twenty-one yet!—and that our story was just another thread in the fabric of turbulent young love.

I wouldn't say I developed intimacy issues after David, at least not in the sense I would contend with after Roy. In fact, I did the opposite. I fall hard and fast—something I'm prone to do in relationships—almost bordering on the obsessive. Obsessive as in "why do I know his cousin's name and occupation?" Instead of withdrawing myself, I used my sadness to springboard myself into the nightlife scene, which was punctuated by bouts of self-destructive behavior. I drank more, did drugs left and right, so much so that, in retrospect, I'm amazed I'm still alive.

I went and slept with an old friend of mine who I knew liked me. Then I started dating someone ten years older than me, not realizing that I was being an asshole who just used both of these men who were genuine in their feelings for me. I was a mess. I hooked up with a handful of other dudes at various clubs and bars, both at Hofstra and in Manhattan, in an effort to forget about David, WHICH TOTALLY ALWAYS WORKS.

In a way, I suppose I did have a set of intimacy issues, except opposite of the ones I was dealing with now. I was abusing intimacy, using it as a weapon that hurt others along the way, all in a vain attempt to protect myself from the pain and sadness I was actively ignoring.

It wasn't until I met Roy, two years later, that I would be forced to examine my relationship with sex.

As my first year in grad school ended, I still wasn't ready to be in a relationship again, but I was ready to have casual sex. I wanted to have casual sex. I knew it was out there. My friends were having it all the time. There are apps designed just for that purpose, like Grindr. Being out of sexual commission for so long yielded some serious sexual insecurities, which is, I guess, a subgroup of intimacy issues. My relationship to sex, like most of my relationships to men and things like fitness, was complicated.

The logistics of casual sex freaked me out. Was I horny beyond belief? Yes. Could I just go out to a gay club and find someone to go home with? Of course. Was I regretting not getting Apple Care for my sex drive? Absolutely. My sexts to men I've met on apps like Tinder and Scruff have gotten so graphic that even PornHub would make the "time out" motion with its hands if it read them.

You know when you sext someone such graphic things, and then when you meet them you're Mother Fucking Teresa, like you didn't just tell them the other night over text that you want them to pound you like a judge pounding their gavel in a courtroom that's in perpetual disorder, and then when you go to meet them in person for the first time and you're all Holier-Than-Thou and you have ash on your forehead and it's not even Ash Wednesday? GUESS I SOMEHOW FORGOT TO FACTOR IN THAT THE WHOLE FACE-TO-FACE THING IN MY PURSUIT OF COITUS.

How was I going to take the next step and actually seal the deal? I was terrified of meeting someone at a bar and then going home with them only to have to explain why I'm half-hiding behind their Oriental room-divider while they sit there naked and ready to get down to business. I wanted to be spontaneous and have adventurous sex—like doing it in a used car dealership—but I couldn't. I knew that even if I tried, I would panic and freeze up and no one would have any fun.

Jumping back in the sack wasn't as easy as I thought it would be. Because of my anxiety, even meeting someone for a drink takes a lot out of me. I need *at least* six hours to lie in my room in the dark and listen to some fucking Enya to try to get myself to calm down. Mind you, this is just to go have a drink with someone. If I know there's a possibility of engaging in coitus with this person? Now we're talking douching—shooting water up my goddamned asshole—which is already in and of itself a production. Now, on top of my usual I'm-going-to-throw-up-at-the-thought-of-meeting-some-one-and-being-forced-to-engage-in-conversation-that-isn't-boring anxiety I'm faced with OH-GOD-DON'T-SHIT-ON-HIS-DICK anxiety.

So already it's taking me a lot out of me just to put on pants and leave the house where there's air conditioning and an array of streaming services. Going out to Meet Someone is more of a production than a Celine Dion Vegas show. Next thing I know, four years go by and the only time I get my hair pulled is when it gets stuck between the subway doors on a crowded L train.

Sex still scares the shit out of me. But now, it's for different reasons: I'm worried about aggravating my acid reflex. I refuse to fuck without my neck pillow. But the act itself isn't as anxiety-inducing as it once used to be for me. I'm in a healthy relationship now. My boyfriend is my best friend who loves and supports me on a level that's deeper beyond my understanding.

I met Pete on one of the 14,000 dating apps I had on my phone at the time. I was smitten with him from the get-go: he was cute, hilarious, and willing to spend nine dollars on a piece of cheesecake for me. But most importantly, I was able to open up to him.

I was ashamed of being celibate for so long. I'm fairly certain this comes from some sort of stigma about celibacy. Every time I would hear someone complain about how they haven't had sex in two weeks, I would mentally choke them with industrial-strength sausage links. TWO WEEKS? Please! If I told them how long I had gone without it, I'm sure I would have received a reaction as though I had just told them I had been diagnosed with some terminable illness.

But when I met Pete, he committed to dismantling all the shame I had accumulated over the past four years. He was patient and gentle with me, understanding when I told him I wasn't quite ready to become intimate. After a month of dating, when we finally did seal the deal, we found our rhythm: humor.

Because of the profound overlap in our senses of humor, making sex funny alleviated our nerves and made it enjoyable. I joke about him sending me a Google Calendar invite for a night that he wants me to bottom, so I could plan my meals accordingly. Tooting isn't just taboo, but welcomed, an unexpected but hilarious punchline. If I'm in doggy style I ask him to get that pesky blackhead I can't reach on my own.

We stopped being insecure about our bodies and their functions, learning to work with them instead of against them. I feel safe and supported, especially on days when I have to take a step back because of my depression, anxiety, or a flare-up from my PTSD or any of the other thousand ailments I've been diagnosed with in recent years. But building our foundation—through patience, trust, and a sense of humor—became the key to stop feeling inadequate about my sexual (in)experience. I've learned to stop letting it affect my life—in every aspect: love, social, and sex—and just go at my own pace. I'm lucky to have a partner to hold my hand along the way.

I'm still not the sexual guru I wish I was, like someone who teaches a BDSM for Beginners workshop on the weekend, but at least I can be honest with myself now, and that's good enough for me. At least I can impart this nugget of wisdom when it comes to sex: JUST WHEN YOU THINK YOU'VE ADDED ENOUGH, ADD MORE LUBE.

I'm speaking from experience.

18. EXPEDITE YOUR STATUS AS A TRUE NEW YORKER: A HANDY CHEAT-SHEET

There's a never-ending debate between NYC natives and long-time dwellers. Depending on whom you ask, people will tell you the only true New Yorkers are the ones born here; others place a ten-year minimum of living here to constitute as one. It's like the ancient battle between good and evil: it'll never end. I read a quote in an article in *Time Out* New York that addressed the issue in one, swift sentence: "Being a New Yorker is an endless process of earning it," followed by list of qualities typical of a New Yorker (buying a dollar slice at four a.m., seeing a movie screening in Bryant Park, walking by a celebrity without batting an eyelash, etc.).

Sure, these qualities certainly substantiate your status as a real New Yorker, but I'm about to tell you HOW TO CHEAT. If you live in NYC, I'm going to tell you how to expedite your New Yorker credibility with these loopholes below, then the next time you have this argument with a native, you can whip out this list and shut down whoever is trying to deny your authenticity. Following each loophole is a percentage of how much your New Yorker status goes up:

-Go see a psychic advisor blackout drunk and crying. *(Expedites your real New Yorker status by 35%).*

-Use your yoga mat to stop the subway doors from closing so you can get on the train. *(60%).*

-Put a cigarette out in an intern's Lean Cuisine. *(20%).*

-Fall into an open manhole in the middle of signing an email with "Best,". *(45%).*

-Get brunch-drunk and hail a taxi with a baguette. *(55%).*

-Googling the word "aesthetic" while sitting in a communal dining area that has white walls and furniture that can only be described as "fun." *(60%).*

-Answer a Craigslist ad for someone looking for another person to practice their knife throwing act on because you're a hundred dollars short with rent. *(45%).*

-Arrive at a job interview with the faint remains of a club stamp on your hand. *(25%).*

-Smuggle granola bars into SoHo House when your friend who has a membership invites you because you know you can't afford the food there. *(15%)*.

-Apologize to your co-worker via email for complicating things and live your professional life in mild discomfort. *(30%)*.

-Fuck your co-worker! You met someone new and cuter and now you're in a happy and healthy relationship with someone who is completely attracted to you, has no emotional baggage, and remembers things like how you like your coffee. *(0%)*.

-Start a start-up. *(55%)*.

-Dip your hair in fake blood and whip your head back and forth at the High Line during peak tourist hour. *(30%)*

-Agree to pay an extra four dollars for three drops of CBD in your latte. *(25%)*.

-Get drunk and hijack a horse carriage with your friends in Central Park. *(45%)*

-Crack your iPhone screen swiping left on Tinder too fast. *(30%)*.

-Move to LA. *(100%)*.

19. TEN TIPS FOR DATING IN NYC

It's no secret that mobile dating apps and astrological compatibility fuel the dating scene in New York City. My publisher and I want to get in on the NYC dating advice gravy train and relationship guide mania, so, I, Greg Mania, will guide you along the path of finding True Love in the big city.

In NYC, dating is *expedited*. Think of it this way: Dating everywhere else: priority mail. Dating in NYC: Express shipping. It's not like anyone in this city actually has the time to get to know you, silly! I don't even have the time to throw out my dead succulents, let alone find out if you prefer one sugar or two in your coffee.

Dating is stressful enough as it is. Let me help you.

Tip #1: The first step to dating—anywhere, really—is to meet someone! There are a TON of places to meet people in this city such as a bar, networking event, or an S&M-themed book club meeting. Remember, first impressions last the longest. If you make it past the first date (recent studies state that's a one in ten chance of that happening in NYC), you can start to dress more casual. You can whip out those fun and flirty Boyfriend Jeans, or if you're feeling *really* saucy, Middle-Aged-Divorcée-Rediscovering-Herself Daisy Dukes or Single-Dad-Lookin'-For-Love-In-All-The-Wrong-Places Classic Bellbottoms. Time will tell.

Tip #2: You want to actually make sure it's a date. New Yorkers often confuse "hanging out" with "dating." A lot of people in NYC seem a little jarred by calling something a "date" and often substitute the phrase "hanging out" to alleviate any pressure they may feel comes with a nascent relationship. Personally, since many of the men I pursue are scared to use the word "date," after I "hang out" with them I scream: "SURPRISE, THIS WAS A DATE" and then I tip my cab driver an extra twenty percent to Tokyo-drift away for embellished effect. This establishes that we were on a date and, more times than not, establishes there won't be another!

If you want to make sure you are in fact on a date when you make plans with someone ask yourself these questions: Did they dress up for a nice evening out? Did they pick you up at your place? Did they bring you flowers? Did one of you pay for both of you? Did they kiss you goodnight after dropping you off at home? Did they call you the next day to tell you how much fun they had last night? Did you go out with them again? Did they sleep over this time and dance the naked tango with you? Did you meet their friends? Did you go back to their place, dance the naked tango, and then stay over for breakfast the next morning? Do they text you good morning? Do they text you good night? Do they text you, "WHO IS THIS PERSON THAT LEFT A WINKY FACE UNDER THE COMMENTS OF ONE OF YOUR SELFIES?" Did they meet your friends? Did you leave the city for a few days to go on a mini- vacation together? Did you fart in front of them without immediately wanting to fake your death and move across the country? Did you meet their family? Did you two argue about something insipidly poignant? Did they meet your family? Did you move in together? Did they find your G-spot? Did they propose? Did you say yes? Did you get engaged? Did you get married? If you answered, "yes," to these questions, it was a date!!!

Tip #3: First dates are super important in NYC, because you usually know if you want to pursue any sort of romantic engagement approximately seventeen to twenty-five minutes after meeting someone. Like I said, dating in NYC is extremely time conscious so be sure that you can foresee a future with them within an hour. When you go on a date, have a star chart ready to go. Ask them what their sign is and see what the future has in store for you as dictated by the cosmos because duh, how the fuck else would you know if you're compatible with someone?

With normal dating you usually know what the person's intentions are, romantically, based on several important things discussed, so get the stuff that you would usually talk about on the third date out of the way on the first date by asking them things like if they have a general disregard for the oxford comma or believe it to be a fundamental building block in sentence structure. Ask them how they would rank the flavors of Starburst (this could make or break a relation-ship!) Next, have them meticulously map out the general trajectory of their five-year plan. Possibly ask for a stool sample.

Tip #4: The first element in a successful first date is conversation. No one wants to hear about what your minor was in college or how you want to try pursuing a creative endeavor involving mixed media. Talk about your exes. As a dating expert, I can tell you this helps facilitate conversation/fun-bitter-revenge-sex. Uncomfortable silences are to be expected, so have a list of topics in case one of those awkward moments come up! Discuss your favorite things to watch on Netflix, a suppressed childhood memory, if you would become a necrophiliac for the promise of one million dollars, the sea, or, if you prefer Beacon's Closet or Buffalo Exchange.

Tip #5: One of the most important components of a date is eye contact. Try to look them in the eye as often as possible. This tells the person you're invested in knowing more about them or possibly have an auto-optical asphyxiation. If they're wearing transition lenses, maintain eye contact with them throughout the entire duration while their lenses catch up and **_DO NOT_** say a word until they do!

Tip #6: This might be looked down upon anywhere else, but it is totally appropriate—and recommended—to pre-game your date. This helps alleviate those pesky butterflies! That's another thing people in NYC don't have time for: BUTTER-FLIES in our ABDOMINAL region! NOT conducive to Soul Cycle! Ugh! Arrive a half an hour early and try to consume between two to four glasses of wine. Remember: it is not appropriate to start blacking out until halfway through your date. Don't feel bad if you get sick, just casually vomit in the nearest appropriate receptacle. A ficus or your neighbor's open Michael Kors bag will do. You need someone to love *all* of you so expose your flaws from the start: admit from the get-go that you're one of those people who hangs the toilet paper roll on the underside, feel free to bring your collection of antique spoons and whip them out before you even order an appetizer, confess that you've been sending your favorite contestant on *Project Runway* a friendship bracelet every year for the past twelve years.

Tip #7: Be warned! There are certain situations that warrant stop, drop and rolling out of the room, and they include, but are not limited to:
- Your date wearing a Bluetooth
- Your date mentioning composting for more than twenty to twenty-five seconds
- A *threatening* fire, I guess?

Tip #8: If you don't hate each other after an hour, you can safely assume you're dating by NYC's standards. And if you do hate them, go into the bathroom and Facebook stalk your ex on your iPhone until they get so uncomfortable that they leave. Relationships take time (WHICH YOU DON'T HAVE), so prepare to resort to alternative methods of getting someone to date you.

Tip #9: Blackmail.

Tip #10: Practice makes perfect! Dating is hard, especially in a densely populated metropolitan area where everyone is too busy making plans that will definitely result in an eternal game of raincheck ping-pong. With practice (and a lot of questionable pharmaceuticals) you'll get the hang out of the dating game here in NYC! If you don't, I thank my therapist in the Acknowledgements. Feel free to look her up.

20. A GUIDE TO BREAKING UP WITH SOMEONE WHEN YOU HAVE A LOT OF MUTUAL FRIENDS

Dating in New York City is a challenge, as we established in the previous chapter. Unfortunately, the greater challenge is breaking up with someone because there's a lot of work that goes into avoiding someone for the rest of your life—especially when the chances of bumping into them in NYC is alarmingly higher than anywhere else in the world. I know what you're thinking: *are the chances really that high in a city of eight and a half million?*

Statistically speaking, the one day you choose to leave your apartment looking even only moderately unkempt, you *will* bump into someone you know, and worse, chances are it'll be someone whose tongue has had a rendezvous with your No-No Area. But what makes it worse is if you have a lot of mutual friends with that person. They'll become inescapable. And thanks to social media you're constantly haunted by where they check-in, what they look like, and their new significant other who is gross and a human landfill and needs to be eliminated immediately.

As you can probably tell from my last chapter, I know my

way around the interminable void that is modern dating in New York City, but my expertise *really* shines when it comes to breaking up, especially when it's someone you know you'll be seeing around because of your overlapping social circles.

Let me tell you a backstory or two that'll help you understand how uncomfortable this situation can be: once I was dating a dude who was serious about No Shave November. I'm not a proponent of No Shave November. I don't want to do a lot of work when I go down on someone. I don't want to use a machete like I'm cutting through thick rainforest undergrowth in a tropical country just to reach a few inches of flesh engorged in blood. I'm not going to bob for dick in November. If I can clip your pubes into a topiary then no deal. I think you get my point.

Look, I'm not saying shave yourself back to prepubescence, but some maintenance is, more times than not, preferred. If I can't see your shaft I'm clocking out. Also, hi, mom. This was just one of the issues with Mr. November; he was also a total lunatic: he declined the cheddar biscuits when we to Red Lobster. WTF. The unfortunate aftermath: we have a lot of mutual friends, so I was constantly hearing stories about him, what he was doing, whom he was fucking, and what unfortunate shade of Manic Panic his hair was that week.

Example number two: I went on a date that was probably one of the most magical dates in my life. We went to a few hole-in-the-wall places that have just the right amount of character that establish them as neighborhood favorites, talked and laughed for hours, and ended the night with a steamy make out session in a subway station while waiting for our respective trains. I thought it went swimmingly. It implied that there would be another date, but when I asked him out on another, he told me that he liked me but didn't know if he could foresee us being in a relationship together. I thought, *you could tell that from just one date?* But instead of being bitter, I was thankful because that inspired the previous chapter. The part that sucked the most was, because of our similar social circles, we attended the same weekly events.

Several other situations followed that rendered many awkward social interactions. I wish I had the nerve to walk in with my head held high and bravely talk to an ex or someone I used to talk to like nothing was wrong but unfortunately, I don't harbor such confidence. Instead, when I'm out and see an ex I immediately retract my head into the papier-mâché turtle shell I wear to avoid awkward small talk. That doesn't mean I'm going to stop going to the places I frequent or stop being friends with people they're friends with—those could be friends willing to share their HBO GO login! If you're like me, lovably uncouth but lacking the social confidence needed to walk into a room with an ex in it without needing to breathe into a brown paper bag, then you're in luck. I've developed a guide to breaking up with someone you thought would jeopardize maintaining a healthy social life:

Breakup Tip #1: You must go through all the stages of a regular breakup. First, there's the initial shock. It's not uncommon to be in denial and harbor the belief that it will resolve itself the next day. More than likely, it won't. Snap back into reality by reading about looming environmental threats. The second stage you might encounter is anger. The healthy way of dealing with this type of anger is to spray-paint "NOSFERATU WAS HERE" in black in their backyard. If they don't have a backyard, have a huge ice sculpture of a liter of Diet Sprite delivered to their apartment for no reason at all. A healthy dose of humor should alleviate some of your anger. The last stage is grief. Allow yourself **NO MORE** than twenty-seven hours to sit outside your ex's area of residence in a car blasting "Bittersweet Symphony" on loop while using opera binoculars to peer into their bedroom.

Breakup Tip #2: You might still be a little emotionally fragile and vulnerable even after going through the common stages of denial, anger, and grief. Beware! Don't let residual overwhelming emotion take advantage of your vulnerability. Remember these adages: don't make decisions when you're angry; don't call when you're drunk; don't show up at your landlord's door wearing a Celtic cloak and nothing underneath when you're lonely. You might not be ready to dive back into your usual social pool yet, especially knowing you might bump into your ex considering your mutual friends and acquaintances. Do little things for yourself. Write down a goal every day like, "today I will go buy a book I've been wanting to read," or, "today I will find myself in a situation that warrants the use of the verb 'vanquish.'"

Breakup Tip #3: Now that you've followed emotionally healthy protocol and centered yourself, it's time to start slowly entering the social world you once knew before some douche lagoon with tattoos and a nice smile decimated it to dust, rendering your desire to do nothing except rent a storage unit that's just for you to scream in. Emotional outbursts are to be expected! That's okay! Embrace them; embrace them with a passion of a thousand burning suns, the enthusiasm of a college freshman at their first extracurricular reading, and the joy of finding out your favorite 90s TV show has been uploaded to Netflix. It may feel a little jarring as you prepare to reenter the world. Your mutual friends are going to pick sides and they're going to keep asking you things like, "when's the last time you spoke to them?" and, "have you stopped sending them dead flowers yet?" Ask your friends to respect during this time and make it abundantly clear that you just want to hang out without talking about the person you broke up with. Gradually ease yourself back into your usual social groove: stick to low-key parties and smaller social functions like an art gallery opening or a Chinese death metal hip-hop show in a storm cellar on the border of Brooklyn and Queens. These are the necessary baby steps you must take before taking the next step.

Breakup Tip #4: Well, it's here. It's time to attend an event where you know your ex will be; it's time to face the music/devil. Sure, you're going to have the urge to fly down to a South American country to have cosmetic surgery that alters your physical appearance, but I assure you that is not necessary, especially if you prepare correctly. Before even attending, acquire the blueprint for the venue you're going to be at. Make note of all exits, including air ducts. It will come in handy in case you see you're corned and see your ex coming towards you and the nearest exit is nowhere but up!

Breakup Tip #5: Now that you're inside first things first: make sure your friends surround you AT ALL TIMES. This decreases the chance of any communication between you and your ex. The more people around you, the better off you will be and can enjoy your night out. Possibly hire some pedestrians off the street if necessary. Now you can enjoy yourself! But always keep one eye open; remain cognizant of the oscillation of people going in and out and make note of where your ex is. If all the necessary precautions you took failed and you're cornered by your ex: REMAIN CALM. After they ask you how you're doing, keep repeating "I'm fine!" while increasing volume until they run away. Trust me, this **never** fails.

Breakup Tip #6 (THE LOOPHOLE): There is one thing you can do that can bypass all these tips: you can just show up to an event your ex will be at with someone new and exponentially more attractive. If you can achieve this, you need not worry about the previous tips regarding preparation and emergency protocol. Unfortunately, if you're like me, it may be a little difficult finding someone new in a certain span of time due to handicapped flirtation skills. Once I tried to court a gorgeous young man riding the subway with me by serenading him with traditional blank verse:

*O BEAUTIFUL MAN PHYSICALLY AKIN TO JUDE LAW ON THE SIX TRAIN WITH SKIN AS GOLD AS THE DYING SUN,
LIPS AS PLUMP AS A TOMATO THAT'S ONLY GOOD FOR ANOTHER DAY OR TWO,
AND HAIR THAT SHINES LIKE A FRESHLY INSTALLED SOLAR PANEL*

He pulled the emergency brake and threw himself through the window. BUT if you do manage to find someone ten times better and more deserving of you, showing up with someone new and significantly more attractive will, if anything, make your ex need this guide more than you! Which is fine. In fact, opt for this step.

See, it's not as hopeless as it seems, right?! Of course, breaking up always sucks no matter what. You're hurt, filled with self-doubt, and prone to exploring arson in your downtime. But there's no need to avoid certain places or people, or go on a self-imposed exile to Qatar. With time and practice you'll get the hang of breaking up with someone you have a lot of mutual friends with, and life will go on as normal (never speaking to them again but staying friends on Facebook).

21. THINGS I WAS ADVISED AGAINST PUTTING IN MY BOOK PROPOSAL SO I PUT THEM HERE

Rejected promotional ideas:

- Tattoo the link to purchase my book across my clavicle.
- Immediately follow a winter release with a spring re-release with a bonus chapter that is entirely scratch n' sniff (preferred scent: Popeyes chicken sandwich).
- Heavily utilize my platform (the actual platform I stand on when I recap old episodes of *The Simple Life* through interpretive dance in the Union Square subway station).
- Share airtime with the next Amber Alert.
- Legally change my name to "Up-and-Coming Writer and Comedian."
- Blimps.
- Good old-fashioned publicity stunt (Have a meltdown on *The View,* wear a cape that says "Ugh, Ryan Seacrest" on the back in Swarovski crystals at a red carpet event, get ranch dressing on a Picasso, etc.).
- Lightly threaten people to buy and promote it (family, friends, Howard Stern).

- Just put "by Amy Poehler" in huge, bubbly font on the bottom of the cover.
- Immediately die after its release.

Frowned Upon Chapter Titles:

- 15 Ways to Vomit with Grace
- Should I Finally Update My Website or Fake My Death?
- Anal in the Age of Plant-Based Meat Alternatives
- Are You Dying or Tired: Take This Fun and Flirty Quiz to Find Out!
- What Your Preferred Brand of Ketchup Says about You
- Here are the Addresses of My Ex-Boyfriends Please Feel Free to Send Them Expired Chocolate and Lab Ants
- Emotional Promiscuity and Me
- Fuck Healthy Salt Alternatives

Things They Called "Misleading" About My Author's Bio:

- Greg Mania is a writer, comedian, and co-wrote *Contagion*
- Mania is frequently asked by popular media to comment on the trendiest disorders to have.
- Greg Mania is also known as his drag alter-ego, Mariska Hargi-Slay.
- "Originally from the Mall of America,"
- Greg Mania is based in the prison of his own mind, help
- "Shortly after finishing his Ph.D,"

22. BABY'S FIRST FLAGRANT DISPLAY OF WEALTH

Okay, I'm exaggerating with the "flagrant" part. And the "wealth" part. It's not like I went out and bought myself a BMW or signed up for automatic billing. But I did get myself something with my first real paycheck doing something in comedy that does have more value to me than anything money can buy. That something was co-writing a movie.

I was already taking a number of screenwriting classes at The New School, and I had already started writing a pilot called *Maniac*, which turned into *Mania* after I found out Netflix was planning to release a show called *Maniac*, starring Jonah Hill and Emma Stone. I was going at it solo, but I thought having a writer partner might be a great way to learn and grow as a writer.

I met Dean Dempsey, in 2013, when I interviewed him for *CREEM*. He had a collection of paintings on display at a gallery in the Lower East Side, and my editor assigned the story to me because she knew we'd be the perfect editorial match. Since she was a good friend of his, she knew that his sense of humor would pair nicely with mine. After meeting the talented painter, I was then introduced to the hilarious writer and filmmaker, when I attended the premiere of Dean's first feature-length film, *Candy Apple*, at the Village East Cinema a year later. I realized that not only were we the perfect editorial match as writer and subject, but possibly as writing partners, too.

I loved *Candy Apple*, so a few days later I shot Dean a message on Facebook, asking him if he'd be interested in having a writer partner. We met at Home Sweet Home, a bar in the Lower East Side, to talk more about possibly collaborating.

I found a genuine soul with a pension for firing one-liners at Phyllis Diller-speed. Of course, I was instantly attracted to the idea of writing with him. He told me he loved the jokes I wrote on Facebook, said that I was the reason he even went online was to read my posts. I was flattered and couldn't believe the moment of kismet unfolding in front of my eyes. Then he showed me how to take a shot of candle wax without burning your mouth. An impenetrable friendship was born.

It was a hot summer night when we were out drinking and playing pool at a dive bar in East Harlem called The Duck. We were in the middle of developing a half-hour comedy pilot called *8 and a Half Million* when his executive producer from *Candy Apple* offered him another movie deal with a budget that was twice the size of his previous film. He asked me if I wanted to co-write the movie with him.

This was big.

Huge.

This wasn't just a big break; this was a real deal. A real *paid* deal. I didn't know if I was cut out for the job.

By the end of the night, Dean convinced me. We decided making a movie together would help usher our pilot into the world. But first, we were going to co-write (and also star in!) a multi-protagonist dark comedy feature-length film that was scheduled to shoot in the fall of the following year.

Everything unfolded perfectly, from pre-production, to casting, to putting together a tremendous and dedicated crew. The schedule was grueling—our call times were often at two or four in the morning—resulting in twelve-hour days for two weeks straight due to budget and location constraints, but we pulled it off.

We await distribution as I write this. Fingers crossed it comes out before climate change renders our planet completely uninhabitable!

And then it came. Shortly after shooting *Deadman's Barstool,* I got my first substantial check for writing something. It was more than three digits. OF MONEY. NOT SEPHORA POINTS OR WHATEVER ELSE I'VE BEEN GETTING PAID IN UP UNTIL THAT POINT. I wanted to barge into the first SoHo boutique I saw with a scepter and proclaim, "I AM RIHANNA. I WILL HAVE ONE OF EVERYTHING."

I couldn't believe it. I didn't even cash the check until a week after I got it because I couldn't stop looking at it and relishing this tangible thing that was a sign that I was finally doing something right and heading in the right direction.

After I finally deposited my check, I decided that I wanted to spend a portion of the money I earned on something that would serve as the reminder of the hard work and the unwillingness to ever give up, despite how many times I wanted to. Sure, I could have put that money into my savings account, but who I am, Suze Orman?! I had already paid my rent and bills with the money I made working as an office assistant because I budgeted for taking two weeks off to film a movie. DAMN LOOK AT THAT SHIT: I just used "budget" as a verb. I fully expect to be listed in the next *Forbes* 30-Under-30 list.

So I did it. I marched into The Cast NYC, a custom leather jacket boutique in the Lower East Side and commissioned a custom-made leather motorcycle jacket in my favorite color: yellow.

My go-to item of clothing is always a motorcycle jacket. In the winter, it's a black leather one; in the fall and spring, it's a velvet one; in the summer, I'll wear my leather motorcycle vest. But I wanted to have a signature piece, a piece that, if I'm ever rendered into a cartoon or a drawing, would always be something I'm seen wearing and therefore remembered by. It's like Hillary Clinton in a pantsuit or David Bowie with a lightning bolt.

I have a very complicated relationship with the color yellow, specifically wearing it, even though it's my favorite color. I believe that there are only three ways to look good in the color yellow:

1. Be Viola Davis
2. Witchcraft
3. Get it custom-made

I'm sure there are some of you who may be the exception to this, and if so, I envy you. But, for me, it has to be a very specific shade, and after all the years I've spent trying to find a leather jacket in this particular shade with no luck, I decided to get it custom-made.

And, at the time, I could afford it!

I went in for a preliminary consultation and I got my measurements taken and picked out all the details: the lining (which is black with red polka dots and even has a patch that says "Mania" on the left breast pocket), the lapels, the placement of the pockets, the fasteners and what tint of silver they would be, waist buckles, the zippers and their placements—it was the whole shebang. I really did feel like Rihanna. (Except I wish that I had to carefully maneuver around an eight-hundred-dollar Givenchy septum nose ring when exfoliating my face in the morning, and whenever I wear an outfit that's just an XL T-shirt, it's less "a look" and more "sir, you can't be in this Olive Garden without any pants on.")

Then came time to pick the color. I was shown a bunch of swatches and the first one I saw was lemon yellow. Here's the thing with lemon yellow: it's in the gold family. I'll never look as good as Beyoncé in the "Hold Up" video so I don't even bother trying with that shade. I was looking for something more in the dusty yellow department. It's sort of like a muted yellow, more on the pastel side. (Forgive me, Morticia Addams.) They had swatches sent to them from a bunch of different suppliers all over the country, and every time I picked a shade I liked, they were, of course, out of it.

I rejected swatch after swatch, but I wanted the jacket to be perfect. I am going to be buried in it, after all. I felt bad for being so picky until they actually invited me to come along to a fabric warehouse in the Garment District to see what kind of leathers they have so I could hand-pick it myself. (I suspect they just wanted me to finally goddamn pick a roll of fabric so they can finally get this jacket made and send me on my way, hopefully never to return again.)

The warehouse was huge, an endless, gigantic maze. Every turn you took had every color, every texture, every style of fabric—it was nirvana. I saw this gorgeous red vinyl-looking fabric and was like oh, there's my next custom-made motorcycle jacket. We finally made our way in the back and my eyes came upon the most optimal shade of yellow I have ever seen. We pulled it out and discovered there was just enough to make a leather jacket in my size.

My prayers to Viola Davis had been answered.

A week or so later, my jacket was finally ready to be picked up. I went to the shop and saw it hanging. It was glorious. I'm not a parent, but I suspect it's like seeing your child for the first time. The color was perfect and it fit me like a glove. And I loved how dramatically the collar popped.

After I left the shop, I walked down the same Lower East Side streets where, just a few years ago, I would probably be walking down on my way to St. Jerome for that evening's Magic Monday; or on my way to see Darian at a party she was hosting around the corner; or helping Ky lug her vinyl records to a party she was DJing. I got the same stares in my yellow leather jacket that I got walking down the streets to those parties, and it almost felt as though nothing had changed.

Except everything had changed.

23. SOMETHING OLD, SOMETHING BORROWED, SOMETHING NEW

I'm writing this chapter in a hotel room in Asbury Park, New Jersey. It's a much different setting than my favorite dive bar in the Lower East Side, where I wrote the first third of this book three years ago. A lot has changed since then: this book has gone from a shabby outline to an actual thing people can use to wedge a door open for a delicate cross-breeze; I live in Brooklyn now; MY BEST FRIEND IS GETTING MARRIED TOMORROW.

That's why I'm here, in my room at the Empress Hotel in Asbury Park, on my third helping of continental breakfast mini muffins, getting emotional. Ky and I participated in NYC nightlife as a unit, from meeting each other at Magic Monday to engaging in hijinks in the Boom Boom Room at the top of the Standard Hotel to hanging out at Ky's neighborhood bar until four in the morning, drinking Rolling Rock and planning our looks for the following night's outing. We've been through relationship after relationship together, one of us always there to pick up the pieces when things inevitably blew up in our faces, for years—wash, rinse and repeat, but with dudes who made us re-blog the same graphic of Joan Jett singing, "I Hate Myself for Loving You," back and forth on Tumblr until the end of time. We didn't know each other as kids, but it still felt like we grew up together.

Now, Ky is marrying Bryan, her wonderful boyfriend of three years now, and I'm the one who will walk her down the aisle.

THIS IS WHY A STATE FARM COMMERCIAL MADE ME CRY THIS MORNING.

My boyfriend, Pete, sits in a chair at the desk that's near the door where our suits hang, catching up on homework. It's almost ten, dangerously close to my bedtime. This is the Greg Mania he knows: the interminably boring twenty-eight-year-old who barely goes out anymore. My interests have moved from bottle service to DIY home improvement. Just this morning, before we left for Asbury Park, I ordered fifty daffodil bulbs online JUST BECAUSE. My garden in Brooklyn, which, by the way, is a generous term, is an old Converse shoe filled with dirt. (I even joined the ADS, the American Daffodil Society, which is the whitest thing anyone has ever done besides, like, you know, colonialism.) My signature sex move is ignoring Facebook invites. It's not that I don't *want* to party anymore; it's just that I *can't*. If I tried to drink even one-fourth of the amount I used to consume during my nightlife days, I'd need at least two to three days to recuperate, assuming that I even survive.

The Greg Pete knows now is very different than the Greg who would pile into his friend Kelle's van in a floor-length faux fur coat, along with ten other friends in varying degrees of wild attire, one of whom would bring an entire bottle of vodka into the car, and drive from the Upper West Side's

Hudson Hotel back to the Lower East Side to continue a night of drunken tomfoolery.

We wake up in the morning and get dressed. We make our way to Porta, where the ceremony and subsequent reception will take place. Pete and I part ways when we arrive, and I join Ky and the other bridesmaids just outside the hall where Pete and the other guests fill the rows of seats. One by one, each bridesmaid and groomsmen take their place until Ky and I are left alone, waiting to make our way down the aisle. We hold hands and wipe the tears that have snuck out of our eyeballs. I make a stupid joke about getting diarrhea right before our cue to enter. Ky tells me to shut up, because we won't hear it if I don't stop talking.

It's time.

We walk out into a crowd of smiling friends and family, camera flashes going off in our faces, and make our way towards Breedlove, who is flanked on both sides by the bridesmaids and the groomsmen. He officiates the ceremony, which is no longer than two minutes long because we all agreed that any ceremony longer than that is a nightmare. Ky and Bryan exchange heartfelt vows with brevity, and we cheer and clap when Breedlove instructs Bryan to kiss his bride.

We file out into the reception area, which is decked out with candles in mason jars, palm leaf and Baby's Breath centerpieces, and a giant gold glittering chandelier in the middle of the room. Dinner is salad, followed by pizza. After we eat and the plates are cleared and the music comes on, Ky and Bryan take to the floor, under the chandelier, for their first dance as husband and wife. We circle around them, watching, as Ash Fox, a beloved nightlife photographer turned wedding proposal planner, takes photos. After their dance we clap and cheer, and Ky immediately runs to me and pulls me in for a dance.

Ky gently rests her head on my shoulder and I lean my cheek against her hair, and for a moment, we just sway to the music as everyone fills the dance floor. I look over at Pete, who smiles as Breedlove says something in his ear. We stay this way for several songs, even as the songs get progressively faster to accommodate the club atmosphere Porta is turning into as evening makes way for night.

Around us, our friend Kat gets so drunk she initiates a dance battle only she participates in. Leah, Ky's sister, does a death drop to RuPaul's "Cover Girl." Breedlove gets prepared to sing a song, like it's 2009 and we're back at St. Jerome, and has anyone seen his prop rotary phone? He can't perform "Love on the Telephone" without it.

It feels like Magic Monday: Wedding Edition.

I tell Ky how beautiful she looks; she tells me that she loves my hair slicked back. We joke about how it's certainly a departure from how we first looked when we met each other in 2010: her with strawberry-blonde hair that was in transition to become a full head of pink hair, me wearing an Axl Rose-style sash around my eleven-inch mohawk. We both agreed that Breedlove's new look is cute, too, his kaftan replaced with a signature varsity jacket; his long hair gone, a buzzed head in its place. He's gone and reinvented himself, just like everyone else at this wedding has, even the ones who weren't there: Darian moved to LA just a few months ago and now lives with Justin Tranter. Justin's solo career as a songwriter has skyrocketed in the past few years, earning him Grammy nominations and a slew of other accolades. Lady

Starlight lives in Berlin. Cecilia is in Edinburgh writing and directing movies. Ky, now retired from working in nightlife, is training to become a cycling instructor at a chic studio in SoHo. I'm taking her class on Monday, and I am already anxious about getting a bike in the back so I can hyperventilate in peace.

Before we know it, what feels like hours have passed. In reality, it was only a few songs, but we remembered that Ky has a husband now, and that I have a boyfriend, and they would both probably like a little attention from their respective significant others. It used to be just the two of us for so long, and we wanted it to stay that way, just a minute longer.

The next morning, in our hotel room, we pack our bags. Check out is in an hour. We laugh as we recount our night following the reception, which started to blur after we left Porta for a nightcap at the hotel bar where Ky and Bryan both had a suite. We'll try to remember who won that game of pool —was it us or Ky's mom and her sister? Did I smoke a cigarette in someone's bathtub? Who was the couple that got into a fight?

We joke about how we should have stayed loyal to our bedtime, that we should have just come back to our room after the reception ended at ten. After swallowing sixty-seven Advil for my pounding headache, I remembered seeing Breedlove say something in Pete's ear yesterday, when Ky and I were dancing. I asked him what Breedlove told him.

After a beat, Pete laughs, remembering. Breedlove had told him a story about the time we were filming the music video for his song "New York Rooftop" in the basement of Ky's old apartment building a few years ago, and we ran out of fog juice for the fog machine. It was almost three in the morning—too late to run out and get more—and we were filming a party scene, the basement filled with thirty of our friends, so we had to finish filming that scene that night. I looked up what fog juice was made out of on my phone, and, when I learned it was primarily made up of glycerin, I poured red Fanta into the fog machine because "glycerin is basically sugar, and Fanta is totally the sweetest soda!"

I laugh because I forgot about that story and OF COURSE MY DRUNK ASS DID THAT. Pete tells me I should use that story for something, like this book or a script. I agree, and while I make a note on my iPhone, Pete tells me he wishes he knew me back then, the nocturnal creature whose hobbies started and stopped at Aqua Net, to see where I came from and how I got to be the person he knows today.

He says he wishes he had met Greg *Mania*.

I wish I had responded with something deep and pensive, some hoopla about how the past is the past, and what matters is the future, BLAH SMEH UGH. Some musing about how, as a writer, my memories are malleable and never far off—all it takes is the right combination of words, peppered with a sometimes painstakingly thought out verb to conjure whatever image I want in your head. Perhaps I could have deployed an elaborate metaphor, calling upon my theater days, when saying "scene" indicates the beginning or end of a scene: it's the start and the stop, going from one end to another and back again, and arriving at the point that growth is more cyclical than linear. But I'M NOT THAT SMART. It took me no fewer than forty-five minutes to come up with that metaphor just now, as I finish writing this book. This book where I metabolize my past, present, and future, sometimes all at once, turning the memories I have made into stories I will continue to tell, promising him that the person he wishes he had known would be introduced to him—to everyone—on page one, and that all you have to do to meet him is go back to the beginning. But being a writer means never having the right words the first time.

So, in that moment, all I said was: you will.

ACKNOWLEDGMENTS

It takes a village. My incredible editors, Leza Cantoral and Christoph Paul, facilitated the growth of this book into the book that it was meant to be. Matthew Revert designed the cover of my dreams. My publicist, Justin Hargett, is a gift. Not only am I indebted to these to folks, I also applaud their patience and ability to put up with my neurosis vis-á-vis email. They're all champs. I want to fill a Gatorade cooler filled with Kindles and dump it over each of them.

This book would not exist without Nikki Maniscalco, who has been there since day one and was the first to read and edit the manuscript chapter by chapter. More importantly, she taught me to believe in this book and myself, and encouraged me to keep writing even when I wanted to give up and become one with the sea.

Thank you to my friends of the best variety: Ky Digregorio, Craig Jessup, Dean Dempsey, Brian Newman, Tommy London, Samantha Irby, Lindy West, Gina Anania, Abby Ringiewicz, Danielle O'Neill, Rachel Lewis, Olive B. Persimmon, Maggie West, Claudia Cogan, John Constantine,

Rebekah Hartie, Tracyann Williams, Jennifer Richards, Ali Greene, Cecelia Perez-Homar, Will Lehnertz, Kirk Rowton, Julie Bashkin, Luisa Schumacher Resto, Ariane Williams, Brooke McNulty, Kristen Rodgers-Anderson, Mike Schin, and friends like Justin T. Moran and Noah Michelson, who, early on, gave my words a home on the internet and encouraged my voice to come out loud and proud.

Katerina Simonova, my friend and first-ever editor, took a chance on me and turned an intern into a professional writer. Lori Zimmer was the person who opened that door for me. They both blazed the path for me and continue to shower me in undying support and love.

I'm not one to challenge Oprah but I will that say my love for teachers rivals hers. Patricia Cregan Navarra recognized my propensity for rebellion and encouraged it. Dr. Mary Ann Allison told me that I had a book in me. I know the latter was expecting this book to be filled with a little more research and a little less dick jokes, but I value your guidance and encouragement just the same.

People tell me this book has "a lot of heart," and I'm like, gross??? I blame my best friend, Rachel Hendershott, whom I grew up with and has witnessed me crying at Applebee's and has never judged me, once. Thank you for teaching me everything I know about being funny and vulnerable. Please don't let my little niece and nephew, Skylar and Alexander, read this until they're at least thirty.

All my love and gratitude to Chuck Guarino and Elisa Maldonado for making my beautiful yellow jacket that I loved so much it's on the cover of this book and has an entire chapter devoted to it. Sorry for being so picky.

My boyfriend, Pete, has gracefully accepted the role of victim by dating me. He's put up with me since the beginning and has hopped on this rollercoaster ride with enthusiasm, always supporting me and reminding me of how proud he is, even for completing the most mundane of tasks, because he knows that some days, even those can be a feat to accomplish for me. But at the end of the day, he offers me unconditional love and support no matter what, and for that, I love him to the moon and beyond.

THANK YOU, LEXAPRO.

Internet friends, specifically the writers and publishing colleagues I've befriended online: I heard you and thanks to your encouragement, I managed to actually do it. This one, and every one hereafter, is for you, always.

To my family, namely Mom, Dad, and Andy: I know there were times when it wasn't easy, but you stuck with me. Thank you for your patience, a quality we all that hasn't been passed on down to me. To my cousins, Robert, Tessa, Jonah, and Izzy: toasting to you all with a can of wine in hand.

And to my other family, the Magic Monday crew: this book wouldn't exist without you. Know that you have touched me and that I wear your fingerprints on my heart like one of my tattoos.

I can't believe how much I love you.

ABOUT THE AUTHOR

© Pete San Pedro

Greg Mania is a New York City-based writer, comedian, and award-winning screenwriter. His work has appeared in *Vanity Fair, O, The Oprah Magazine, Out, PAPER, Electric Literature, The Rumpus,* and *HuffPost,* among other international online and print platforms. This is his first book.

Follow him on Twitter, Instagram and Facebook: @gregmania Website: greg-mania.com

ALSO BY CLASH BOOKS

TRAGEDY QUEENS: STORIES INSPIRED BY LANA DEL REY & SYLVIA PLATH

Edited by Leza Cantoral

GIRL LIKE A BOMB

Autumn Christian

99 POEMS TO CURE WHATEVER'S WRONG WITH YOU OR CREATE THE PROBLEMS YOU NEED

Sam Pink

THIS BOOK IS BROUGHT TO YOU BY MY STUDENT LOANS

Megan J. Kaleita

PAPI DOESN'T LOVE ME NO MORE

Anna Suarez

TRY NOT TO THINK BAD THOUGHTS

Art by Matthew Revert

HEXIS

Charlene Elsby

THE ELVIS MACHINE

Kim Vodicka

WE PUT THE LIT IN LITERARY

CLASHBOOKS.COM

FOLLOW US ON TWITTER, IG & FB

@clashbooks

EMAIL

clashmediabooks@gmail.com